OLD BOOKS AND NEW HI[...]
AN ORIENTATION TO ST[...]
BOOK AND PRINT CULTU[...]

Studies in the culture and history of the book are a burgeoning academic specialty. Intriguing, rigorous, and vital, they are nevertheless rooted within three major academic disciplines – history, literary studies, and bibliography – that focus respectively upon the book as a cultural transaction, a literary text, and a material artefact. *Old Books and New Histories* serves as a guide to this rich but sometimes confusing territory, explaining how different scholarly approaches to what may appear to be the same entity can lead to divergent questions and contradictory answers.

Rather than introduce the events and turning points in the history of book culture, or debates among its theorists, Leslie Howsam uses an array of books and articles to offer an orientation to the field in terms of disciplinary boundaries and interdisciplinary tensions. Howsam's analysis maps studies of book and print culture onto the disciplinary structure of the North American and European academic world.

Old Books and New Histories is also an engaged statement of the historical perspective of the book. In the final analysis, the lesson of studies in book and print culture is that texts change, books are mutable, and readers ultimately make of books what they need.

(Studies in Book and Print Culture)

LESLIE HOWSAM is a professor in the Department of History at the University of Windsor.

LESLIE HOWSAM

Old Books and
New Histories:
An Orientation to Studies
in Book and Print Culture

UNIVERSITY OF TORONTO PRESS
Toronto Buffalo London

© University of Toronto Press Incorporated 2006
Toronto Buffalo London
Printed in Canada

ISBN-10: 0-8020-9438-4 (paper)
ISBN-13: 978-0-8020-9438-4 (paper)
ISBN-10: 0-8020-9196-2 (cloth)
ISBN-13: 978-0-8020-9196-3 (cloth)

∞

Printed on acid-free paper

Library and Archives Canada Cataloguing in Publication

Howsam, Leslie, 1946–
  Old books and new histories : an orientation to studies in book and print culture / Leslie Howsam.

  (Studies in book and print culture)
  Includes bibliographical references and index.
  ISBN-13: 978-0-8020-9196-3 (bound)
  ISBN-10: 0-8020-9196-2 (bound)
  ISBN-13: 978-0-8020-9438-4 (pbk.)
  ISBN-10: 0-8020-9438-4 (pbk.)

  1. Books – History.   I. Title.   II. Series.

  Z4.H697 2006   002   C2006-902210-0

University of Toronto Press acknowledges the financial assistance to its publishing program of the Canada Council for the Arts and the Ontario Arts Council.

University of Toronto Press acknowledges the financial support for its publishing activities of the Government of Canada through the Book Publishing Industry Development Program (BPIDP).

LESLIE HOWSAM

Old Books and
New Histories:
An Orientation to Studies
in Book and Print Culture

UNIVERSITY OF TORONTO PRESS
Toronto Buffalo London

© University of Toronto Press Incorporated 2006
Toronto Buffalo London
Printed in Canada

ISBN-10: 0-8020-9438-4 (paper)
ISBN-13: 978-0-8020-9438-4 (paper)
ISBN-10: 0-8020-9196-2 (cloth)
ISBN-13: 978-0-8020-9196-3 (cloth)

∞

Printed on acid-free paper

Library and Archives Canada Cataloguing in Publication

Howsam, Leslie, 1946–
  Old books and new histories : an orientation to studies in book and print culture / Leslie Howsam.

  (Studies in book and print culture)
  Includes bibliographical references and index.
  ISBN-13: 978-0-8020-9196-3 (bound)
  ISBN-10: 0-8020-9196-2 (bound)
  ISBN-13: 978-0-8020-9438-4 (pbk.)
  ISBN-10: 0-8020-9438-4 (pbk.)

  1. Books – History. I. Title. II. Series.

  Z4.H697 2006   002   C2006-902210-0

University of Toronto Press acknowledges the financial assistance to its publishing program of the Canada Council for the Arts and the Ontario Arts Council.

University of Toronto Press acknowledges the financial support for its publishing activities of the Government of Canada through the Book Publishing Industry Development Program (BPIDP).

Contents

PREFACE vii

1 Disciplinary Boundaries and Interdisciplinary Opportunities 3
2 Mapping the Interdisciplinarities 16
3 Models of the Book's Place in History 28
4 Where Is *the Book* in History? 46
5 Cross-Disciplinary Observations: The Mutability of Texts, Print, and Readings 65

NOTES 79
BIBLIOGRAPHY 93
INDEX 107

Preface

Old Books and New Histories is meant to be an orientation, a kind of field-guide, to identifying and appreciating the three major scholarly approaches to studies in the history and culture of the book. These approaches are made through literary studies, bibliography, and history, disciplines with very different and sometimes conflicting problematics, which converge upon a phenomenon that is simultaneously a written text, a material object, and a cultural transaction – the book. This particular book is an essay addressed primarily to two audiences who will no doubt read it in rather different ways. People who have been practising scholars in this area over the past twenty-five or thirty years will, I hope, be stimulated to reflect upon how theoretical approaches, both familiar and innovative, and the burgeoning literature of the field look when organized and depicted along the fault lines of competing and overlapping academic disciplines. For students, many of whom are now being introduced to the field in one self-consciously 'interdisciplinary' or 'cross-disciplinary' forum or another, this essay attempts to provide some grounding, to show where the subject is coming from, and to explain what perspectives are being adopted, perhaps unconsciously, by their teachers and by the authors of the works they are assigned to read. For all readers I present an array of books and articles, deployed as examples around my argument about the importance of discipline, but each of them worth exploring in its own right.

This book is short, and makes no claim to be comprehensive. Everyone who has read it has suggested adding something, usually from his or her own disciplinary perspective. It is limited by my own experience and expertise: *the book* whose history it investigates is the western book, and, with a few exceptions, the modern printed book. And even when the disciplinary perspective is literary or bibliographical, the stance is still historical. Others will, I hope, take up the study of contemporary book culture from the perspective of the other social sciences; this book is unashamedly a strongly engaged defence of the perspective of the discipline of history upon the history of the book.

Every book has a history of its own, and this one began over twenty years ago when I made two simultaneous discoveries; the first was the joyful recognition that the history of books was an approach to the past eminently suited to someone like me, since I had returned to the discipline of history and entered graduate studies from a work experience devoted to book and periodical editing. The second was more painful, because it came with a twist: at the same time as I learned that many of the contributors to this interdisciplinary discipline were historians, and very distinguished ones (like Natalie Zemon Davis, Robert Darnton, and Elizabeth Eisenstein), I discovered that the history of the book was not a subspecialty that departments of history in even major universities felt obliged to cover. It was the colleagues and friends who made up the Toronto Bibliography Group who were my unofficial seminar in the history of the book: our first shared reading was D.F. McKenzie's *Bibliography and the Sociology of Texts*. By the time I came to enter the academic job market in the early 1990s, I had learned to call myself a cultural historian, because *book history* still seemed to be too rigid, too object-oriented, or too literary for many departments to embrace. But since 1993 my colleagues and friends at the University of Windsor have given me the opportunity first to realize myself as a historian among historians, and then to research and teach the history of the book with renewed enthusiasm.

Still the question of disciplinary boundaries continued to trouble me. I offered a paper to the conference of the Bibliographical Society of Canada in 1995, and another five years later to the Society for the History of Authorship, Reading and Publishing, meeting in Mainz on the (presumed) anniversary of Gutenberg's birth. Bill Bell, of the Centre for the Book in the University of Edinburgh, organized a panel where I was the historian among four scholars of various disciplines addressing the question 'where is book history?' We planned to put together a volume with essays from our different disciplinary perspectives, but the pressure of other commitments made this impossible to complete. My own contribution to that intended book (many more books are imagined than ever are written) has now been revised and expanded to become *Old Books and New Histories*.

After a brief introduction that sets out the field of studies in book culture and its three core disciplines, chapter 1, 'Disciplinary Boundaries and Interdisciplinary Opportunities,' draws a triangle with one academic field at each corner. Chapter 2, 'Mapping the Interdisciplinarities,' fills in the triangle with examples from the literature. In chapter 3, 'Models of the Book's Place in History,' the graphic and other theories proposed by Robert Darnton, by Thomas R. Adams and Nicolas Barker, and by Peter MacDonald are reproduced, discussed and critiqued, and a new approach is adduced from James A. Secord's work on the convergence between the histories of the book and of science.

Chapter 4, 'Where Is *the Book* in History?', moves away from the disciplinary triangle to the discipline of history itself, asking and answering its own question with reference to the historical problematic of agency, and then to that of communication in past cultures, looking at the history in which books have their part along the dimensions of time, place, and change over time. Finally chapter 5, 'Cross-Disciplinary Observations: The Mutability of Texts, Print, and Readings,' concludes that from all three disciplinary perspectives the lesson of studies in book and print culture is that texts change, books are mutable, and readers make of books what they need.

A word about the endnotes: I have been concerned to maintain the balance of the text of this essay, and to avoid overwhelming any one section with extensive passages from the works cited, or with lengthy discursions on matters of specialist interest. Such materials have been consigned to the notes, which constitute what McKenzie once referred to as 'a literal sub-text.'

My chief academic debts are to Jacqueline Murray and James Raven, who in their different ways have taught me what it means to be a historian. After them comes Niklas Holmberg, my research assistant for this project, who set to work energetically and with great intelligence to discover models and theoretical approaches to the history of the book that I might have overlooked. An astonishing number of scholar-colleagues have been generous enough to read every single word of the manuscript: Germaine Warkentin, Yannick Portebois, Heather Jackson, Gail Chester, Shelley Beal, and Jennifer Connor. The manuscript was read for the University of Toronto Press by David Hall (who graciously revealed his name to me), by an anonymous reader, and by a member of the Manuscript Review Committee. All these nine readers' comments have been incorporated in the book, much to its benefit. Jill McConkey of the University of Toronto Press has been a strong supporter from the beginning. Others whose help I am glad to acknowledge are William Acres, Nicolas Barker, Bill Bell, Fiona Black, Pierre Boulos, Joan Bulger, David Finkelstein, Patricia Fleming, Janet Friskney, Juliet Gardiner, Scott Green, Rosemary Halford, T.H. Howard-Hill, Finola Hurley, Yvan Lamonde, Mary Lu MacDonald, Suzanne Matheson, Kathleen

McCrone, David McKitterick, Jacques Michon, Robin Myers, Kristen Pederson-Chew, Barbara Porter, Barrie Ratcliffe, Jonathan Topham, Bruce Tucker, David Vincent, Ian Willison, and finally my students in both graduate and undergraduate book-history courses at the University of Windsor. The university's Humanities and Social Sciences Research Grant paid for much-needed research assistance.

Neil Campbell, finally, has been a source of strength and insight; he is the only genuine general reader of my acquaintance, and the first, last, and best reader of everything I write.

Windsor, 2006

OLD BOOKS AND NEW HISTORIES: AN ORIENTATION TO STUDIES IN BOOK AND PRINT CULTURE

1

Disciplinary Boundaries and Interdisciplinary Opportunities

This little book introduces the reader to the study of book and print culture by situating that study within the several scholarly disciplines that converge to make it up. It is meant to help new students orient themselves within the field, as well as to provoke discussion among veteran scholars.[1] The study of book culture is so wide-ranging as to be inherently disorienting. It has to do with written communication in its diverse forms and processes. Its practitioners think about the reception, the composition, the material existence, and the cultural production of what is called *the book* only for lack of any better collective noun. The book is not limited to print (it includes manuscripts and other written forms), or to the codex format (periodicals and electronic texts come under examination, as do scrolls and book rolls), or to material or literary culture. This vast scope and these blurred boundaries mean that no one can ever be an expert on all its aspects. Indeed, for many practitioners an intense interest in generalities can exist alongside a certain unease concerning their ignorance about particularities. As one of my students once concluded, 'the book is a shape-shifter,' and the attendant condition of disorientation can be both pleasurable and disturbing, intoxicating and mind-altering, creative and confusing. Perhaps because of this condition one scholar argues that 'readers need to stand somewhere before they pick up a book.'[2]

One of the places we stand is in the academic discipline within which our minds are trained.

The three core disciplines that converge upon the study of book and print culture are history, literary studies, and bibliography – the fields of study that focus respectively upon the book as a cultural transaction, a literary text, and a material artefact.[3] The interdisciplinary approach draws upon all three, and each core discipline connects with one or more related fields of study. Hence the disorientation, because all these disciplines assert their own theoretical assumptions and methodological practices, and each one changes as new generations of scholars challenge their predecessors. All of them contribute to an account of communication and cultural connection that revolves around the written word. Such a narrative tells the story of people in community, disconnected in time and space and yet also tenuously united by their shared experience of reading a book or other text, perhaps a whole genre or oeuvre. No doubt that communal experience of reading is shaped largely by the individual (or the collaborative group) who composed the text, but the apparent primacy of authors may obscure a denser reality. Studies of book culture seek out the connecting tissue between readers and writers and ask questions about relationships. Who inspired this book's composition, and who intervened to change and distort and revise the words and the material form that in turn influenced people who used it to shape their world view? What of those who made their living by producing the artefact, by marketing it, or by managing its disposition in libraries? Can knowledge of the mechanics of the trade help us puzzle out the motives of readers? Is it possible to get closer to the thinking of those among our ancestors who used this book for their own purposes – for political change or material gain, for national identity or private solace, or for the stimulation of intellectual, spiritual, aesthetic, sensual, and other appetites? Can we find a way to recognize the bookishness of things that we do not initially recognize as books? Studies of book culture use a wide range of scholarly methods and disciplinary approaches to attempt to answer these questions.

Although interdisciplinary studies of book culture are flourishing at the beginning of the twenty-first century, and perhaps because such courses and programs have become popular in universities, the nomenclature of the field remains contested. *The book* is often cast as an unfamiliarly abstract term and collective noun, identified as a phenomenon, like a nation or an idea, that has a recoverable past. Like social class (in E.P. Thompson's famous formulation), the book is not so much a category as a process: books happen; they happen to people who read, reproduce, disseminate, and compose them; and they happen to be significant.[4] *The book* can be a force for change and *the history of the book* documents that change. This powerful usage, derived from the French (*l'histoire du livre*), strikes the Anglophone ear a little oddly. While writing and reading are concepts whose history implies process rather than object, to identify the book this new way embraces both, and further recalls the mechanisms of production and distribution that connect them.

The most commonly used term is *the history of the book* (or simply *book history*). It has recently been noted that 'this label is somewhat misleading, though, since "the book" in this context can signify almost any sort of text: nonbook as well as book, script as well as print, nonverbal as well as verbal.'[5] The histories of writing and reading reach backward and outward, far beyond the introduction in fifteenth-century Europe of printing with movable types, but for those whose interest focuses on post-Gutenberg periods in the west the compelling term is *print culture*, which encapsulates the material nature of the printed word as well as its cultural context. It privileges such ephemeral forms as newspapers and periodicals equally with the apparent solidity of bound volumes and accords advertisements as much attention as canonical texts. But print culture carries its own temporal limitations, ignoring not only the production and circulation of manuscripts since ancient times but also the intellectual problems inherent in coming to terms with electronic texts. The contingent nature of the book is sometimes signalled by breaking it down into its component processes and speaking instead of a history of authorship, publishing (with bookselling and libraries), and reading. Others who wish to contemplate present as well as past, material as well as abstract, find the words 'history' and 'culture' equally troubling and prefer to speak of 'book studies.'[6]

Practical questions are also relevant to the interdisciplinary politics of the academic study of book and print culture. As Cyndia Clegg has remarked, 'an interdisciplinary discipline poses some problems.'[7] The history of books, as we shall see, is not a subject in the history departments of many universities, at least in North America. In some departments of English and other languages the offset from literature per se and literary theory may make the study seem unwarranted and its practitioners unwelcome. Communications studies and similar programs may be focused on the broadcast media, with little time or faculty expertise devoted to the written word. And some approaches to cultural studies are inclined to be impatient with the empirical zeal to which book culture scholars are devoted. Both students and teachers need a place where they can recognize each other by what Robert Darnton once called 'the glint in their eyes' and a metaphorical secret handshake.[8]

No term is quite right, not even *studies of book culture*, because the studies in which we are engaged tend to break down common definitions and shatter familiar images. The written text in its well-known codex form (defined by the 1982 *Concise Oxford Dictionary* as a 'portable written or printed work, filling a number of sheets fastened together, usually with sheets sewn or pasted hingewise and enclosed in a cover') seems to be one of the most concrete artefacts that has survived intact from the past. But the first lesson students learn is to mistrust the apparently changeless or fixed 'nature of the book.'[9] Whether handwritten, printed, or digitized, the book's apparent solid materiality conceals the quality of malleability. That is what makes it interesting, though it must be admitted that the paradoxical nature of the book also makes the study of it one of the more rigorous, demanding, and competitive of humanistic endeavours.

Practitioners of the study of book culture often find themselves defending their work against those who have proclaimed the death of the book. That premature announcement has sometimes been derived intellectually from Roland Barthes, who spoke of the death of the author, and from Michel Foucault, whose work problematized the persona of the author and indirectly suggested that it is just as valid to ask what a reader made of a work as what the author intended.[10] Criticism from another dimension is articulated in the strident claim of those computer and Internet aficionados who insist that a medium in which they have themselves little interest (and of which they have less knowledge) will be superseded by new technology, in spite of the evidence of thousands of years of practice and habit, scholarship and experience. Book-lovers are driven to such acts of defensive humour as the sham advertisement for a 'major technological breakthrough!!! – the new Built-in Orderly Organized Knowledge device called BOOK.'[11]

Book-lovers in the scholarly world have discovered their own defences. Far from being an outmoded and dreary form, the book is a challenge to the humanistic imagination. D.F. McKenzie has observed that 'what we much too readily call "the book" is a friskier and therefore more elusive animal than the words "physical object" will allow.'[12] But the scholarly potential (a duller way of speaking of that frisky and elusive quality) of the historicity of books is not self-evident. A recognition that the study of book cultures needs to be defended is a good starting point for the analysis of its border tensions. Why, after all, should scholars of any discipline problematize anything about that familiar printed object, so commonplace as to be almost invisible? Most historians, like almost everyone in the academic world, have a dual working definition of the book as both a convenient source of orthodox ideas and established information and also the ideal vehicle, still convenient, for circulating new ideas and fresh information. The convenience is magnified when the book is our own. If we possess a copy, either as mere owner, or in the special sense of possession implied by maintaining a book collection, we can consult it freely, write in the margins with impunity, shelve it as a trophy, sell it, lend it, or give it away. And even the most modest of scholars has a collection of reference works and key monographs written or edited by his or her peers and available for consultation. If we claim authorship, the book is our own in another sense. For scholarly writers a published book is the result of painstaking research and cogent analysis, first distilled into a unique text and then multiplied for distribution. Among humanists at least a book published by a reputable academic press remains the primary notch on our curricula vitae. And notwithstanding the Internet, a book with its complex arrangement and layers of argument remains our most highly valued mode of scholarly communication. But, like almost everyone, most academics take books for granted, even the ones we write. Students of book culture interrogate contemporary as well as past practice, and they make their contemporaries aware of books and other media as the material and commercial and cultural artefacts that happen to support the texts they are reading.

Disciplinary Boundaries and Interdisciplinary Opportunities

The study of book history is characterized as 'interdisciplinarity run riot' in Darnton's influential 1982 article. A few years later John Sutherland remarks that 'publishing history ... lacks binding theoretical coherence. Territorially,' he observes, 'its status is Balkan, opportunistically annexed when convenient by history, bibliography, economics, sociology, literary criticism, library science.' More recently Michele Moylan and Lane Stiles sound the same note in their introduction to *Reading Books*, referring to book history as a field 'oblivious to methodological and theoretical boundaries,' while Clegg wonders 'if addressing disciplinary questions of history of the book is not somewhat gratuitous.'[13] Riotous interdisciplinarity, territories vulnerable to annexation, contested or undefended boundaries – the language of conflict is interesting, and troubling. Perhaps, after nearly two decades of energetic practice, the time has come to examine the situation. A more subdued metaphor, invoking diplomatic negotiation rather than public disorder, might be more useful. If studies of book culture are to be the methodologically and theoretically rigorous practice they can be at their best, some attention is in order to the boundaries they negotiate. The three humanities disciplines that form the core of historical studies of book culture – history, literature, and bibliography – may be conceptualized as points on a triangle, as illustrated in figure 1.

Although history was once known as the Queen of the Humanities, its arbitrary position at the top of the triangle in figure 1 is not a claim of primacy, even among equals. This is a triangle susceptible to rotation; it is a matter of perception, not of primacy or superiority, and its concern is the question of where particular projects and specific approaches intersect with others. The left side of the triangle manifests what any first-year liberal-arts student learns about the difference between history and literature: in the crudest terms, one is about events in general, while the other is about a particular set of peculiar events that take the form of written works. While historians use written and other evidence as primary sources with which to construct secondary accounts of the past, literary scholars are concerned with works of art which, in Jerome McGann's words, 'recreate – they "stage" – a world of primary human intercourse and conversation.'[14]

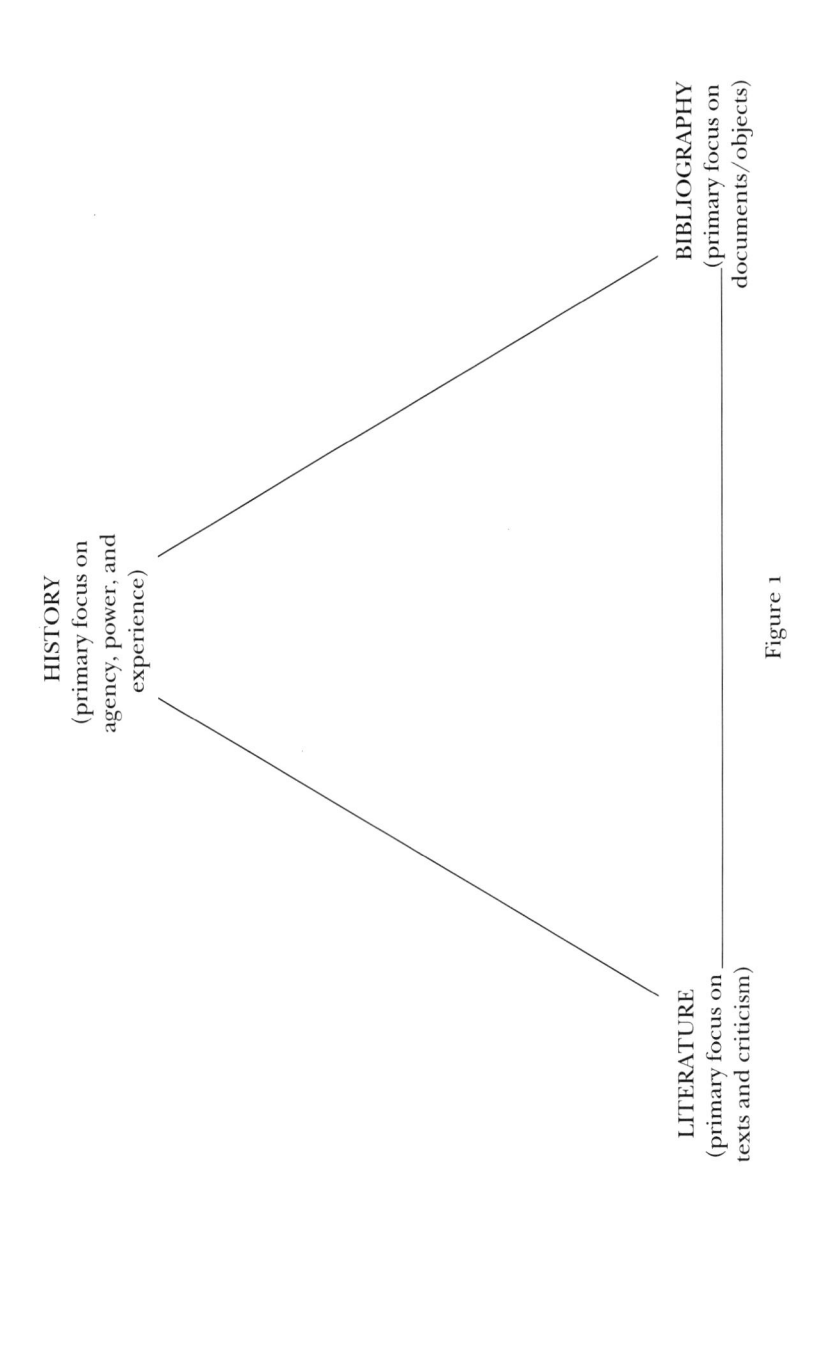

HISTORY
(primary focus on agency, power, and experience)

BIBLIOGRAPHY
(primary focus on documents/objects)

LITERATURE
(primary focus on texts and criticism)

Figure 1

Literature
Literary studies of both past and present, as ways of understanding the human condition, are approached by means of reading literary texts and learning the skills of criticism. Although the concept of a literary canon has come into question in recent years, students of literature still read, discuss, and are helped to understand a body of written work within which each work is characterized as forming part of a genre and as taking its place in a network of influence and allusion. Students are expected to develop a familiarity with the works of genius identified by their culture, from Beowulf to Virginia Woolf, as the expression goes. But works (or texts) in the abstract cannot be separated from the material forms in which they appear, are used, and survive.

Various trends in literary studies over the years have placed more or less importance upon the cultural context for literary texts. People who studied literature in the New Criticism decades of the 1950s and 1960s were discouraged from any examination of outside influences, whereas the contemporary interest in the materiality and cultural specificity of texts has created a very different atmosphere. Confusingly, though, one manifestation of this latter approach is called 'the new historicism' although it has little to do with the research-oriented practice of most historians.[15] This and other ways of thinking about the complexities of literary texts are discussed in *Theories of the Text* by D.C. Greetham.[16]

History
In historical studies and history courses the same broad humanistic dimensions are approached by a different problematic, where the trajectory moves sequentially through time within a specified place, as the tag line 'from Plato to NATO' suggests. Ludmilla Jordanova points out, in *History in Practice,* that history is not a body of knowledge at all, but rather 'an abstract idea with many meanings,' which may

be manifested chronologically, geographically, ideologically, or thematically.[17] Students of history learn to think about what happened in a particular place, or to a particular group; they contemplate why those events matter, and how things change over time. The range of 'things' that change over time and come within the academic historian's purview has expanded in recent years, no longer being limited to political matters – constitutions and laws, wars and revolutions. Nor is the leadership of great men implicitly granted the courtesy of being identified as the driving force, or agency, in historical change. Practitioners have expanded the discipline's range of concern about the past to include matters of social class and gender, and also of identity in terms of race, ethnicity, and nationality. So students might take courses on the history of Germany or Europe, of Costa Rica or the Americas, on the history of African-Americans, of women's movements, or of sexuality in the middle ages. The cultural historian Judith Walkowitz identifies the 'analytic categories conventionally of interest to the historian: power, agency, and experience.'[18] In her study of sexuality and violence in late-Victorian London she shows how these categories can be deployed to address human relationships in communities. These same analytic categories can equally well be deployed to deal with such other sites of cultural contest as the histories of authorship, of publishing, and of reading.

Jordanova has identified cultural history as one of two forms in which contemporary historians now attempt to write 'holistic history' or '*histoire totale*,' that is, to establish a framework for writing a broad-brush and yet accurate narrative about a period, of short or long duration, in the past. The other is biography; in *History in Practice* Jordanova suggests that 'taking a person as the unit of analysis is to adopt a quite particular historical approach, one that emphasises individual agency and sees the subject as a point at which diverse historical forces converge, while taking the span of a human life as a natural period of time.' When the person under analysis is a writer, or a reader, an examination of the book culture in which he or she exists will be an important element of a biography. Cultural history, Jordanova continues, is a 'manifestation of the wish for forms of history which recreate the range of experiences and imperatives to which all human beings are subject.'[19] Some ambitious experiments in the history of the book are similarly finding in the material text a point where diverse historical forces converge. James Raven's *London Booksellers and American Customers*, for example, 'pursues a conception of cultural history as a sum total of past ideas and practice rather than as a residual category of social history.' And James Secord's *Victorian Sensation* explores 'the introduction of an evolutionary account of nature into public debate in order to see what happens when a major historical episode is approached from the perspective of reading.'[20]

Bibliography
Students may have to wait until they enter a program in library and information studies, or perhaps do graduate work in literature, to be introduced to the third point on the book-history triangle, the discipline whose concern is with the book as a material object. Even then only a fortunate few will encounter the study of bibliography, where the emphasis is on the preservation and transmission of written texts.[21] The trajectory here is from scroll to codex (and perhaps to e-text) as well as from manuscript to print. Virtually every copy of every early printed book is unique, differing in small or large ways from others even in the same edition. Bibliographers, whether they are antiquarian booksellers, librarians, or academics, know how to interpret the evidence that books carry within and alongside their texts. When the text matters, these variants and scholarly inferences about their causes can be used to solve problems of textual authority. When the reader matters, the focus shifts to reconstructing his or her experience of the page design and the material quality, as well as the idiosyncratic marks

left behind in the margins and upon the flyleaves of books that have passed through many hands. When the printer or publisher matters, evidence is sought in the patterns of production, down to the watermark of the paper mill and the chemistry of the ink. Sometimes the only way to find out about one of these elusive aspects is to approach it by investigating evidence that survives for one of the others. On rare occasions documentary evidence has survived external to the book itself. But even without letters or ledgers the culture of the past can be reconstructed from books alone.

With the transition to machine printing and the adoption of other new technologies in the early nineteenth century the patterns of production became somewhat more regular. Still it was not only possible, but commonplace, to make changes, sometimes dramatic ones, whenever the book was reprinted while letting the title page and other material aspects of the book appear untouched. As in the hand-press period, these disparities can reveal significant evidence of contemporary thinking. The same bibliographical skills apply: close examination of multiple copies, with an eye to variation. An example is to be found in Herbert Spencer's influential 1873 book, *The Study of Sociology*. Published in the International Scientific Series by Henry S. King and later by Kegan Paul, Trench, the book sold an impressive 26,330 copies having been printed in successive issues of 1250 copies each. Although the text was stereotyped and remained unchanged, the publishers allowed Spencer the opportunity to revise the notes: he took advantage of this to 'carry on an endnote battle with William Ewart Gladstone, who had objected in a public lecture and later in print to a slur on Christianity in the concluding chapter.'[22]

To emphasize the difference between conceptualizing the book as (material) object and the book as (literary) text or (cultural) transaction, it is useful to cite Thomas R. Adams and Nicolas Barker's terminology of the object of study, the book, as a 'bibliographical document – something printed or written in multiple copies that its agent, be it author, stationer, printer or publisher, or any combination thereof, produces for public consumption.'[23] Here is the historians' category of agency (although the related ones of power and experience are notably absent). 'Text' scarcely comes into this definition, either, and the reading public or the broader culture is cast in passive terms ('for public consumption'). Adams and Barker's agent is the person who used pen or type, with ink, to inscribe the paper or parchment that has survived to be studied. For the bibliographer, then, the primary focus is on the document, or on the book as physical object, and the social context in which it emerges drops to the background.

Students of bibliography learn the skills of analysing and describing a book in such a way as to identify its distinguishing marks, the traces its makers have left behind. As D.F. McKenzie argues:

> By dealing with the facts of transmission and the material evidence of reception, [historical bibliography] can make discoveries as distinct from inventing meanings. In focussing on the primary object, the text as a recorded form, it defines our common point of departure for any historical or critical enterprise. By abandoning the notion of degressive bibliography [that is, of finding an abstract ideal version of a literary text] and recording *all* subsequent versions, bibliography, simply by its own comprehensive logic, its indiscriminate inclusiveness, testifies to the fact that new readers of course make new texts, and that their new meanings are a function of their new forms.[24]

The comprehensive logic and the indiscriminate inclusiveness of bibliographical scholarship are remarkably powerful, astonishingly particular, and (like the powerful logic and particular methods of history and of literary studies) difficult for the uninitiated to grasp.

2

Mapping the Interdisciplinarities

Many of the projects in which people who identify themselves as students of book and print culture are engaged can be located somewhere within the disciplinary triangle. A few examples, not meant to be comprehensive, are suggested in figure 2.

History/Literature

When the historian is engaging with literary analysis, the result may be a project of cultural history. In a discussion about the relationship between literary studies (including literary history) and historical studies Ludmilla Jordanova remarks that 'cultural power resides not in authors but in their products, rendering it misleading to name and speak of authors, since they do not, cannot, determine or control how their products are read and used.'[1] This comment on the practice of history in the contemporary academic milieu might well be cited as a rationale for using the history of the book as a methodology for cultural history. One fine example is Scott E. Casper's *Constructing American Lives: Biography and Culture in Nineteenth-Century America*. In that work Casper is 'interested in recovering the American experience of biography, not simply a neglected genre.' Part of this recovery is to 'propose what a cultural history of

HISTORY
(primary focus on agency, power, and experience)

BIBLIOGRAPHY
(primary focus on documents/objects)

cultural history
literary history
print culture studies
cultural studies
women's studies
reception theory

history of a single book
publishing history
book-trade history
imprint bibliography

sociology of texts
authorship/composition studies
readership studies
(single-)author bibliography

LITERATURE
(primary focus on texts and criticism)

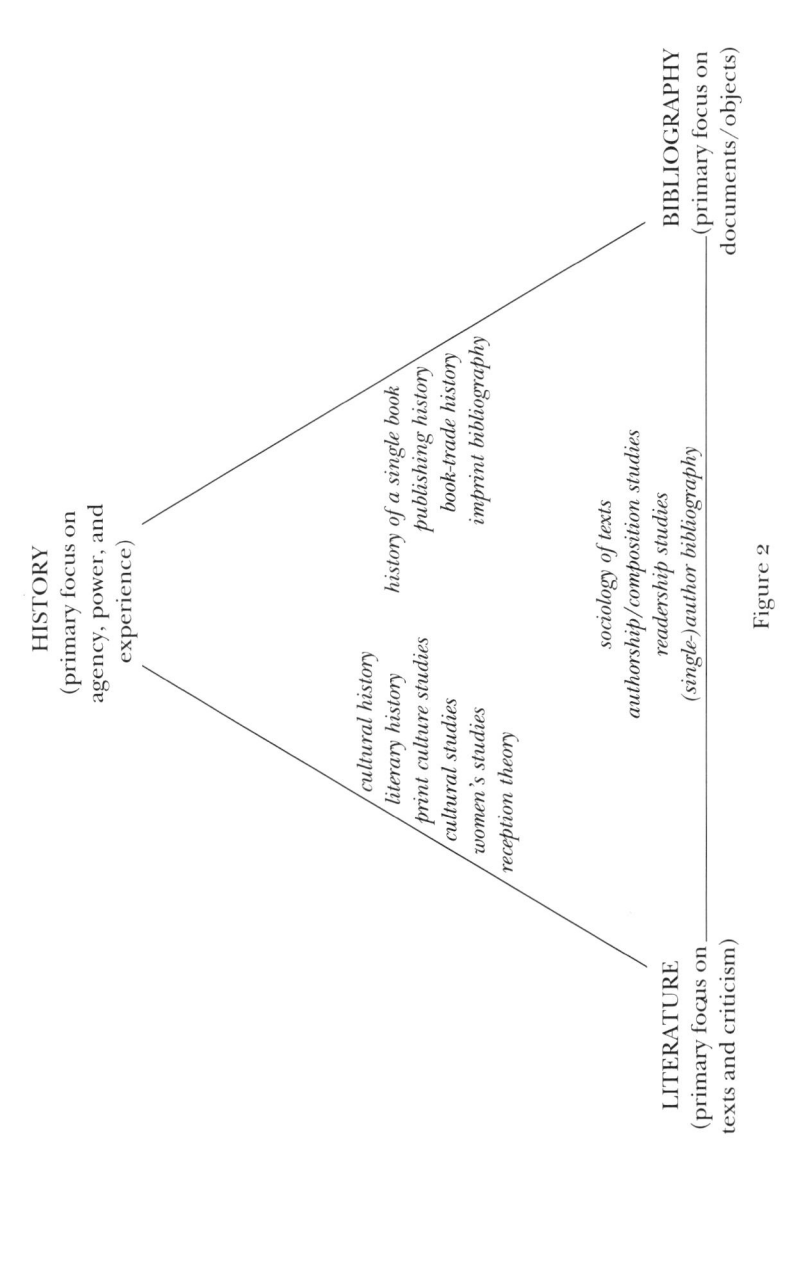

Figure 2

genre might look like,' and even to 'introduce actual readers into the discourse of genre.'[2]

Another literature/history approach is literary history itself. As David Perkins has remarked, literary history differs from history per se in that it 'is also literary criticism. Its aim is not merely to reconstruct and understand the past, for it has a further end, which is to illuminate literary works.'[3] Although some literary historians restrict their research to issues of authorship, others include a consideration of the material culture in which such works emerged and were used. Margaret J.M. Ezell in *Writing Women's Literary History* has shown that, contrary to Virginia Woolf's imaginary portrait of a beleaguered Judith Shakespeare, 'seventeenth-century women did indeed participate in literary circles,' but their work was circulated within coterie networks, in manuscript, apart from the contemporary culture of print.[4]

As we have seen, the concept of a print culture is a powerful (though contested) notion.[5] A volume of essays published in 1998, *Print Culture in a Diverse America*, generated a collection of studies about a nation that was diverse in ethnic, racial, and gender terms; the contributors' several methods and approaches to print culture history recovered the cultural memory of lost or forgotten print, mostly newspapers or other periodicals, sometimes books, associated with such groups as African Americans, women, migrants, and immigrants.[6] Print culture can be recovered from the perspective of readers too, or, as Jonathan Rose calls them, 'audiences.' Rose argues in his book *The Intellectual Life of the British Working Classes* that when working people wrote their own history (as autobiography), they wrote extensively about their experience of reading. The autodidact culture of nineteenth- and early-twentieth-century England was a culture of print.[7] And in a very interesting recent book by Meredith L. McGill, *American Literature and the Culture of Reprinting, 1834–1853*, we learn that despite the cultures of printing in antebellum Philadelphia, New York, and Boston there was 'a flourishing trade in cheap, reprinted British books, which, because unconstrained by copyright, achieved remarkable national distribution in the form of competing, regionally produced editions.' Rather than ignore these books because they were not written by Americans, she reflects that they were read by Americans, and argues that 'the proliferation of cheap, reprinted texts and the reliance of the book trade on periodical publishing realigned relations between author, publisher, editor, and reader, upended the hierarchy of genres, and troubled the boundaries of the text-as-object.'[8]

Cultural studies and women's studies also appear along this axis of the triangle, although these also intersect with other disciplines, notably sociology and anthropology. They represent what might be called the contemporary history of the book, where such phenomena as popular reading groups and Internet bookselling are the subject of study.[9] Janice Radway's important study *Reading the Romance: Women, Patriarchy and Popular Literature* was originally conceived as a contribution to feminist sociology; in the study American women who, during the late 1970s, enjoyed and sought solace in romance novels were interviewed and taken seriously, their pleasure in reading explained by feminist theory.

When the critic of literature is engaging with the discipline of history, his or her project might be focused on reception theory.[10] The questions asked by reception theorists have been characterized by David Allan: 'Is the impact of a text determined not at the moment of its composition, but by the disparate contexts in which it is read? Might its intellectual and literary significance be the creation – or even the re-creation – of readers and audiences rather than of the author? And what considerations might shape the reader's construction – or, again, his or her reconstruction – of a particular text's meaning?'[11] Other disciplines are sceptical about the possibilities of finding 'the reader in the text,' to quote the title of one important collection: we have already seen that D.F. McKenzie says bibliography 'can make discoveries as distinct from inventing meanings,' – as distinct, that is, from theorizing what the text reveals about the author's imagined reader. And some scholars would prefer to seek out the surviving archival evidence of readers' responses rather than resort to theory. It is disconcerting but exhilarating to contemplate the notion that readers to some extent make the meanings of the texts that authors create, rather than authors altogether determining the meaning of the books that readers encounter.

Literature/Bibliography

Moving around to orient history and literature with the third point of the triangle, a good place to start is with Roger E. Stoddard's startling assertion that 'whatever they may do, authors do *not* write books. Books are not written at all. They are manufactured by scribes and other artisans, by mechanics and other engineers, and by printing presses and other machines.'[12] Bibliographical studies of literary works have examined and compared the diverse material manifestations of some literary texts, including the chief works in the western canon. When an author as important as Shakespeare has left nothing behind to verify his intended words – except a variety of irreconcilable products of artisanal manufacture – there is a strong motivation to work backwards from the material object to the author's intentions. Such work may be fragmentary and inconclusive, but it is the scholarly basis for many of the literary works we study and perform today.[13]

Perhaps the most compelling statement of a link between literature and bibliography is McKenzie's formulation of bibliography as the discipline that investigates 'the sociology of texts.' With their focus on the materiality and specificity of books bibliographers locate literary and other texts in their social context. Observing in a celebrated essay on literacy and print in early New Zealand that 'it is ... the bibliographer's job to show editors (and historians) how rich an account of human behaviour the physical elements of a book may yield to those who *can* read all its signs and so recreate the historical dynamics of its making and reading,' McKenzie points towards a new relationship between bibliography and literary studies.[14] This is a contextual approach that signals a shift 'from questions of authorial intention and textual authority to those of dissemination and readership as matters of economic and political motive and of the interaction of text and society as an important source of cultural history.'[15] McKenzie turns the relationships of bibliographical and literary studies inside out, and in the process makes a place for historical and cultural approaches to the book.

In a similar vein, in their introduction to a collection entitled *Reading Books: Essays on the Material Text and Literature in America* Michele Moylan and Lane Stiles argue that 'when we read books, we really read *books* – that is, we read the physicality or materiality of the book as well as and in relation to the text itself.' They and their contributors go on to explore 'the relationship between materiality and meaning, between book and text.' They acknowledge the early contribution of Cathy N. Davidson, whose 1989 work, *Reading in America: Literature and Social History*, 'offers a model for those scholars who want to connect – really, reconnect – the worlds inside texts with those outside; the gateways for these connections are books themselves, which in their varying morphologies and manifestations encode the histories of the texts they embody.'[16]

Another case where literature is not purely literary, nor bibliography purely bibliographical, is in studies of the authorship or composition of novels or poetry. Work in this vein on Victorian England has been particularly rich: Robert L. Patten's 1978 study of *Charles Dickens and His Publishers* is now recognized as a founding text in this area; newer works include those of Jerome McGann and Peter L. Shillingsburg.[17]

Readership studies (like print culture studies) differ from reception theory in being more likely to seek the reader's notes surviving in the margins of the material text, or in her diary or his commonplace book, than to discern a theorized reader in the text itself. Allan's article on the history of reading in the context of the Scottish Enlightenment elegantly states the central problem:

> It remains a peculiarly troubling thought for historians that so much of the evidence they employ to reconstruct the past serves much better to describe the actions of long-dead persons than to tell us why and with what degree of insight they performed them. The historical method often seems a revision of the old adage that one can lead a horse to water, but one cannot force him to drink: whilst one might describe how a horse is led to water, one invariably remains unable to say what is going through its mind when it refuses to drink. ... Only the ... fragmentary and widely dispersed evidence left by direct engagement with the book – by its actual consumption, rather than merely by its formal ownership – can eloquently testify to the reader's own experience as he or she not only received but ... 'appropriated' the text.

Allan makes a compelling case for the 'potential of the commonplace book as a resource for the history of reading – even, perhaps, for a social history of ideas.'[18]

Another rich resource for the histories of reading and of ideas is to be found in the margins of books where readers recorded their immediate responses. H.J. Jackson has shown how extensive and how revealing such records can be. 'What used to be considered a negligible form of writing' is now of central importance to the literary scholar who shares Jackson's interest 'in interpretation and in the *progress* of interpretation, both in the individual reader and in the great society of readers over time.'[19]

An ambitious recent contribution to the history of reading, though in a different key, is William St Clair's *The Reading Nation in the Romantic Period*. His 'reading nation' is Great Britain and his 'Romantic period' is about 1790 to 1830. The argument, which revolves around the creation, management, and deployment of a literary canon, stretches back to Caxton and forward to the twentieth century. St Clair proffers a nested set of assumptions: 'To help to understand and trace the possible effects of reading on mentalities, we need to trace historic reading. To trace readership, we need to trace access. To trace access, we need to trace price. To trace price, we need to trace intellectual property, and to trace intellectual property, we need to trace the changing relationship between the book industry and the state'.[20] Other scholars have stressed the importance of price to the reader's access; St Clair highlights the significance of intellectual property.

Finally, and more traditionally, author bibliography also appears here. Books by a single author (or sometimes by a coherent group of authors) are the focus of analysis. The bibliographer lists them, by title and by date, and produces accurate descriptions that distinguish carefully among the various editions. Canonical authors whose works have been edited to a scholarly standard, and whose books are regarded as collectible, have often been the subject of a bibliography. Dan H. Laurence has illustrated the kinds of literary and political knowledge that can be had from examining how subsequent editions differ from the first. The collector of first editions of George Bernard Shaw, for example, would deprive himself of

> the enjoyment of reading, in the 'second edition' of Shaw's novel *An Unsocial Socialist*, the taunting letter from its protagonist Sidney Trefusis to the author; the alternative prologue to *Caesar and Cleopatra*; the polemical preface to the Home Rule edition of *John Bull's Other Island*; the added chapter in *The Perfect Wagnerite* and its significant preface to the first German edition; the commentary on Ibsen's four important last plays in *The Quintessence of Ibsenism*; and the chapters on Fascism and Sovietism in *The Intelligent Woman's Guide to Socialism and Capitalism*. Moreover, the poor benighted soul would, alas, never know that Eliza Doolittle was going to marry Freddy.

Laurence shows how a bibliography can be woven into 'a unique tapestry: into a biobibliographical portrait of an author in the workshop, the printshop, the bookshop.'[21] Although a multiple-author bibliography cannot go into the same depth as Laurence's work on Shaw, or Richard L. Purdy's on Thomas Hardy, a well-chosen focus can prompt reassessment by bringing together well-known and forgotten writers. One example is *Women Writers of the First World War: An Annotated Bibliography*.[22]

Bibliography/History

Whatever the specific approach, studies that focus on the book culture of a particular place and time are usually both bibliographical and historical. They come out of a cross-disciplinary perspective elegantly expressed by McKenzie in terms of a history of meanings: 'The new forms we give to texts in the acts of adapting, printing and publishing them constitute the most basic and ubiquitous evidence we have for a history of writing and a history of meanings. Every extant artefact tells a tale which we can read historically and which, by virtue of the *edition* (multiple copies of the same forms widely dispersed, successively altered, and variously directed), supports a high level of historical generalisation.'[23] Ian Green's work on *Print and Protestantism in Early Modern England* is a brilliant example of what can be done by a historian working with the *English Short Title Catalogue* and hence with a richer-than-usual tranche of pamphlets and other publications. Green focuses neither on the canonical nor on the very cheapest books, but rather on best-sellers and steady sellers, 'on those works which sold best and most consistently over a period of decades.'[24]

Along the history/bibliography dimension we can locate the study of a single book, where scholars use archival as well as bibliographical evidence to situate the composition, production, and reception histories of a particular work in the culture where it emerged and survived. Earlier examples include Robert Darnton's *The Business of Enlightenment: A Publishing History of the Encyclopédie 1775–1800* (1979) and my own *Cheap Bibles: Nineteenth-Century Publishing and the British and Foreign Bible Society* (1991). A recent contribution to this genre is *Victorian Sensation: The Extraordinary Publication, Reception, and Secret Authorship of 'Vestiges of the Natural History of Creation'* (2000) by James A. Secord, which is discussed further below (41–5).

Various kinds of publishing history also fit into this dimension. Critical studies of publishing businesses bring out the commercial aspect of literary culture. One fine example is Michael Winship's study of the business of 'the preeminent publisher of belles lettres, especially poetry, in the United States of the mid-nineteenth century.' Winship uses the firm's surviving business records to examine in detail 'how Ticknor and Fields operated in the historical world in which it existed, and how it participated in the literary and book trade institutions of which it was a part.' Similarly David Finkelstein in *The House of Blackwood: Author-Publisher Relations in the Victorian Era* combines the examination of balance-sheets with the close reading of correspondence and memoirs to produce an illuminating study.[25]

Book trade history, for Britain, has been written by Peter Blayney in detailed studies and mappings of the history of the Stationers' Company. A series of conferences organized by Robin Myers and Michael Harris has resulted in a number of distinguished volumes of book trade history. The 2003 volume on 'topographies of print' demonstrates 'how the topographical structures of the trade within the dense and confusing urban spaces can be established, and how particular forms of commercial activity are linked directly to their spatial organization.'[26]

The bibliographer who is oriented more to the social, economic, or political dimensions of the past than to its literary aspect may compile an imprint bibliography, painstakingly seeking out every single variant of every single text that fits within the chosen parameters. One such work emerged from a collaboration of scholars examining a past economy and culture from the perspective of literary labour: *The English Novel 1770–1829: A Bibliographical Survey of Prose Fiction Published in the British Isles.* Where general editors James Raven, Peter Garside, and Rainer Schöwerling and their contributors found 'a disordered literary history' there now exists 'a new historical and sociological profile of the popular novel and popular novelist of the period.'[27] Another example, more historical than literary, is Patricia Fleming and Sandra Alston's revision and updating of Marie Tremaine's 1952 *Bibliography of Canadian Imprints, 1751–1800.* Their volume adds many new titles and '[redefines] imprint to include the whole production of the press, from books to printed blanks.'[28]

Despite its richness, the history of the book is not *l'histoire totale,* nor is all historical, literary, and material-text scholarship reducible to the study of book and print culture; some of it remains discipline-specific. The vast majority of scholars in all three core disciplines (as well as all the related disciplines) manage, of course, to get through very distinguished lives and careers without identifying themselves as historians of the book. Each point of the triangle is, in turn, a node on some other taxonomy of approaches to the discipline in question.

Nevertheless, those whose concern is with text in cultural context will find themselves engaging with the resources, and encountering the theoretical preoccupations, of the other two branches of scholarship. My purpose in emphasizing, perhaps overemphasizing, disciplinary boundaries that exist in studies of book and print culture is not to suggest that every scholar learn the methods and problematics of all three disciplines. Rather, it is to appeal for mutual respect. In Cyndia Clegg's words, 'to practice interdisciplinary scholarship ... requires a certain humility in the face of long traditions of bibliographic, historiographic, and critical practice, and a willingness to acknowledge and incorporate these precedents along with often unaccustomed methodologies.'[29] The real differences among the three approaches sometimes lead to derisive commentary that can be read as offensive. We shall see below, for example, a historian who jokes about students of the material text as if the study of watermarks were intrinsically elitist or antiquarian, and a bibliographer who appropriates to his own discipline the whole project of that of historians. Two literary scholars have playfully characterized book history as 'the new boredom' ('bound up in a paleopositivism, content with a set of boring exercises ... cordoned off from the sexier knowledges in academe') while a self-identified book historian has written off the whole literary theory enterprise as worthless.[30] Such attitudes are unhelpful in an interdisciplinary enterprise. Different disciplines ask not only different questions, but different kinds of questions. When disciplinarities converge upon the study of texts, print, and books in historical context, the differences are apt to be contentious, but also enlightening. Roger Chartier in *The Order of Books* addresses the question of how people in the past developed 'operations that made it possible to set the world of the written word in order.'[31] Historians, bibliographers, and literary scholars order their approaches to the book in history, but in different ways.

3

Models of the Book's Place in History

All three terms – history, literature, bibliography – are robust concepts that resist being limited by a single profession's expertise, or indeed by the practices of an academic discipline. Historians have no copyright on the word 'history,' nor students of literature and ideas on 'the text,' nor scholars of bibliography and library studies on 'the book.' This chapter first describes the way in which the book's place in past cultures is conceptualized, or modelled, in a seminal article by one historian, Robert Darnton. Then it discusses three critiques that have emerged in the more than two decades since Darnton's article first appeared, one by a collaborative team of bibliographers, one by a literary scholar using cultural theory, and one from the history of science.

Robert Darnton: The Communication Circuit Model (1982)

The initial assigned reading in many university courses in the study of book history or print culture is Darnton's 'What Is the History of Books?' – an article first published in 1982 and reprinted many times since, without authorial revision but sometimes truncated by editorial abridgment.[1] Darnton answers his own question in the title not by defining 'books' or 'history' but by suggesting that this 'important new discipline ... might even be called the social and cultural history of communication by print ... because its purpose is to understand how ideas were transmitted through print and how exposure to the printed word affected the thought and behavior of mankind during the last five hundred years.' And not only by print: manuscripts and other forms are included, but Darnton is primarily concerned with demonstrating how ideas, embodied in printed texts, circulate in a given society, from author to publisher and printer (and others in the book trades), to bookseller and other distributors, and on to the reader, whose influence on authors serves to 'complete the circuit,' and ensure that 'books do not merely recount history; they make it.' Darnton sketched the development of what he identified as an innovative and promising field of study, one that '[seemed] likely to win a place alongside fields like the history of science and the history of art in the canon of scholarly disciplines.' Significantly his much-cited model (see figure 3) is followed by an extended example from eighteenth-century French history because, in Darnton's words, 'models have a way of freezing human beings out of history.'[2]

Darnton's expressed concern about the profound differences of ideological point of departure and of disciplinary and methodological assumption in the field of book history has already been cited. He suggests that it has begun to look 'less like a field than a tropical rain forest, ... so crowded with ancillary disciplines that one can no longer see its general contours.' Darnton concludes that 'to get some distance from interdisciplinarity run riot, and to see the subject as a whole, it might be useful to propose a general model for analyzing the way books come into being and spread through society.'[3] Darnton proposes his model of a circuit of communication in order to circumvent this clamour of interdisciplinarity. He drafts it as a way of showing 'some holistic view of the book as a means of communication [which] seems necessary if book history is to avoid being fragmented into esoteric specializations, cut off from

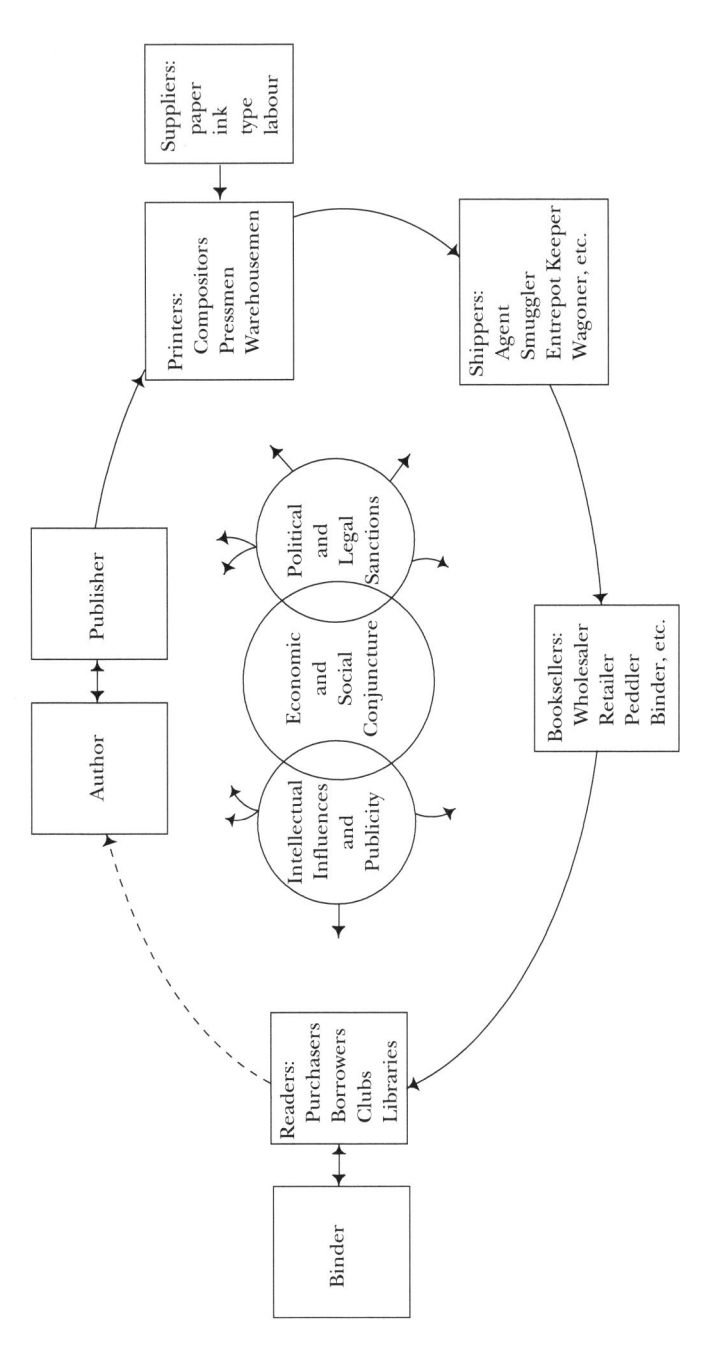

Figure 3 From *The Kiss of Lamourette: Reflections in Cultural History* by Robert Darnton. Copyright © 1990 by Robert Darnton. Used by permission of W.W. Norton & Company, Inc.

each other by arcane techniques and mutual misunderstanding.' The communication circuit 'runs from the author to the publisher ... the printer, the shipper, the bookseller, and the reader. The reader completes the circuit, because he influences the author both before and after the act of composition.'[4] Each node in the circuit is related to a variety of factors, notably other elements in society. These related elements Darnton places in the centre of the diagram: the economic and social conjuncture; intellectual influences and publicity; political and legal sanctions.

The analogy with an electrical circuit – closing, firing, connecting – is particularly arresting. Darnton's model is one of communication, of relationships between people mediated not by the text they all read but by the book trade practices of a given time and place. His *book* is as much an abstraction standing for those mediated relationships as it is a physical artefact.

This approach sets Darnton in the scholarly tradition of *l'histoire du livre*, as practised in French universities.[5] He had associated himself more directly with this approach in the introduction to *The Business of Enlightenment* (1979). There he called for a fusion of the French social-history approach with the Anglo-American tradition of analytical bibliography. Despite his anxieties about creating mutual misunderstanding, he inadvertently insulted some scholars of bibliography by drawing a contrast set in a rare-book room, peopled with 'aficionados savoring bindings, epigones contemplating watermarks, *érudits* preparing editions of Jane Austen, but where you will not run across any ordinary, meat-and-potatoes historian attempting to understand the book as a force in history.' The contrast was between the work of historian-generalists and bibliographer-specialists: 'the generalist could learn a great deal from the specialists in the treasure houses of books. They could teach him to sift through their riches and to tap the vein of information that runs through their periodicals.' Darnton claimed at the time that French research neglected 'the processes by which books were produced and distributed,' and hoped that a mixture of 'British empiricism with the French concern for broad-gauged social history' would produce 'an original blend of the history of books.'[6] A great deal of the work done in the last twenty years has indeed been inspired by Darnton's thinking, although it must also be said that a great deal of that inspiration has taken the form of resistance to the idea of the book as a circuit of communication.

Darnton's remarks drew criticism at an early stage from G. Thomas Tanselle, a distinguished proponent of that same Anglo-American tradition of analytical bibliography. Sidestepping any comment on the communication circuit, Tanselle instead chided Darnton for making a distinction between bibliography and history. Nor was he open to the suggestion that the scholarship of the former field of study is something remote and secondary, which can be tapped by the practitioners of the latter. On the contrary, Tanselle insisted strongly that bibliography is a 'fully-fledged branch of history itself.'[7]

Tanselle's claim, unproblematic to many practitioners of his own discipline, sounds incongruous to the professional historian. In contemporary universities in Europe and North America the major branches of the historical profession are normally designated as political, social, and economic history; some of the newer-fledged branches, now flourishing, are women's and gender history, the histories of ethnicity, race, and national identity, and cultural history. Darnton's historian colleagues are unlikely ever to accept the notion of bibliography as a branch of history, but they are open to persuasion of its utility as a method to be borrowed from a cognate discipline. Although chapter 5 of this essay suggests some preliminary approaches, historians' confidence in the utility of bibliography will, in the end, have to rest upon a body of persuasive scholarship. Meanwhile the historians whose history concerns books share with Darnton an understanding of human agency, of communication in historical context, of the book as a kind of 'transaction' by which 'the written word made public' is created, circulated, received, and reformed.[8] James Raven, for example, calls for the history of the book to 'be sufficiently broad to allow a history of communication and of social and political transformation that goes beyond the immediate inception and reception issues of books.'[9]

Thomas R. Adams and Nicolas Barker: A Book-Centred Model (1993)

A critique of the Darnton model by Thomas R. Adams and Nicolas Barker inverts the relative importance of material artefact and human practice. Adams and Barker are bibliographers; they call their 'New Model for the Study of the Book' a manifesto. They welcome Darnton's work, along with Elizabeth Eisenstein's *The Printing Press as an Agent of Change*, and the new popularity of the book as a subject of study. At the same time they are concerned to identify the historians' intervention as an encroachment upon an established discipline, bibliography: 'The bibliographer, his field of study thus unexpectedly dragged into the limelight by academic historians, has reacted to exposure on the wider stage with mingled fascination and alarm.'[10]

Adams and Barker's article is conceived as a 'chart' for the 'task of blazing a trail' and exploring 'a common path forwards.' They articulate their concern that bibliography has for many years been 'treated as an ancillary discipline [to literary studies], in service to the higher goal of establishing an accurate text.' They regard as a turning point the 'celebrated statement' of D.F. McKenzie in his 1969 article 'Printers of the Mind' that 'the essential task of the bibliographer is to establish the facts of transmission for a particular text, and he will use all relevant evidence to determine the bibliographical truth.' Such evidence includes printing and publishing house archives when they survive, and the evidence of other books being printed at the same time as the one in question. Thus, they continue, with McKenzie's influential article 'the activities of literary bibliographers shifted focus from the purity of the text to its transmission.'[11] Or in McKenzie's own words, they abandoned the notion of degressive bibliography. So far, so good.

Adams and Barker then move on to the 'Statement on the History of the Book' drafted at an international conference in 1980, which refers to 'all aspects of the history of production, publication and distribution, from the stage of authorship on through to the impact of books on readers and, ultimately, on society.' For Adams and Barker one word in this statement signals a problem: 'It is in the insertion of the word "ultimately" that we see the influence of social historians emerging. The statement would have been just as strong an assertion of the importance of the history of the book without it. With it, bibliography again becomes ancillary to social history, again a "handmaiden" to another discipline.' They ask: 'Is the study of books to be doomed to perpetual servitude to all others?' And they answer themselves: 'The subject is important enough to be recognized as something that stands by itself ... It does not apply a specific discipline (such as history or physics) to all events, but all disciplines to specific events, in this case books.' Like Tanselle, they seek to enhance the status of bibliography as a scholarly discipline, and to protect it from those who would relegate it to an auxiliary role. They detect in Darnton and others the appearance of 'a patronizing tone ... suggesting that the work thus far done isn't "real" or important history.'[12]

There is much in Adams and Barker's model to commend it, but nevertheless the bibliographers who are expecting historians to take seriously their approach to the history of books are making some rather large assumptions and demands. One is similar to that of their colleague Tanselle, who also wanted bibliography to be accepted as a branch of history. Another is to put objects at the centre of inquiry, in place of either human activity or abstract concepts of discourse and communication.[13] Nor are these disciplinary tensions reduced by bibliographers' reversing the direction of condescension and noting that, although social historians 'are not writing the history of the book,' they can nevertheless 'make important contributions to it.'[14]

What emerges from this confrontation between history and bibliography is more than 'interdisciplinarity run riot.' Adams and Barker offer an articulate defence of the boundaries between two disciplines, but it is one that mitigates against realizing the ideal of a fully cross-disciplinary scholarship. In their model (see figure 4) they enter directly into competition with Darnton's communications circuit, pointing out quite correctly that 'it deals with people rather than with the book. It is concerned with the history of communication,' and thus, 'for those who are concerned with the total significance of books ... it has limitations.' They propose an alternative scheme:

> a circle of connected elements which are influenced, or can be influenced, by the forces placed in the centre. But since our theme is the book rather than the people involved in its movements, the order of Darnton's elements and forces is inverted. The cycle of the book becomes the centre: the indirect forces are seen outside it, looking and pressing inwards. Instead of the six groups of people who make the 'Communications Network' operation we have five events in the life of a book – publishing, manufacturing, distribution, reception and survival – whose sequence constitutes a system of communication and can in turn precipitate other cycles.

As opposed to Darnton's metaphor of the electrical circuit, which is closed when writer and reader influence each other, Adams and Barker regard their scheme as a 'map,' in which decisions about arrangement, about what to place in the centre of the world, suggest 'relationships rather

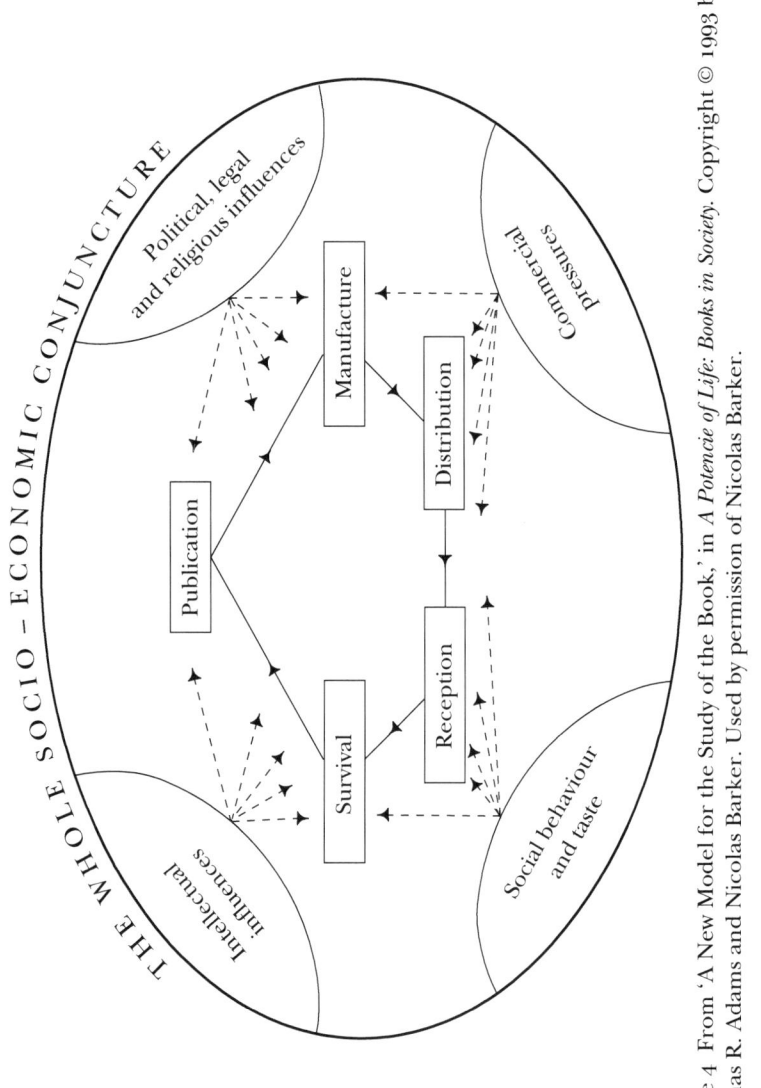

Figure 4 From 'A New Model for the Study of the Book,' in *A Potencie of Life: Books in Society*. Copyright © 1993 by Thomas R. Adams and Nicolas Barker. Used by permission of Nicolas Barker.

than exact locations.' Most striking is the establishment of publishing, not authorship, as 'the point of departure.' For these commentators, as for Roger E. Stoddard, 'the decision to publish, not the creation of the text, is ... the first step in the creation of a book.'[15]

Although the metaphor of a circuit is apparently dynamic, and that of a map static, Adams and Barker nevertheless put their finger on a serious weakness of the Darnton model. In his model the book self-destructs when it has served its purpose of communicating between reader and author. The collector, who acquires the book more with the intention of preserving it than of reading it, whether for an institutional collection or a private library, is treated no differently from any other purchaser. And yet the forces influencing the survival of printed materials are crucial in determining a later generation's perceptions.[16] The bibliographers' model also allows for the tenacity of books, their tendency not only to survive in their original form but to undergo transformation into new editions, revisions, translations, abridgments, retellings, and other formats, all of which are in turn subject to their own patterns of survival and transformation.

Adams and Barker's protective comments on attempts to situate the book as a force in history, however, reveal a disciplinary barrier higher than those raised by cultural historians or literary scholars, both groups by now accustomed to poaching in the methodological and theoretical preserves of their colleagues in the humanities and social sciences. The curiously gendered terminology of bibliography serving as a 'handmaiden' to history, as it has long done to literary studies, is not only suggestive of a certain anxiety about independence and about the relative strengths and weaknesses of disciplines and subdisciplines; it also serves as a reminder that, unlike history and literary studies, bibliography has experienced very little analysis in terms of social class and almost none in terms of gender, race/ethnicity, or national identity.[17] These theoretical questions that have rocked other parts of the academy have left bibliography relatively unscathed.

Peter D. McDonald: A Critique from Literary Studies (1997)

The effect of questions of class, race, and gender upon literary studies has been profound. Students of English and other literatures have turned to a number of different theoretical approaches in order to approach literary texts, both canonical books and other narratives hitherto excluded from the conventional literary canon. In *British Literary Culture and Publishing Practice 1880–1914* Peter D. McDonald takes Darnton's model and makes it three-dimensional. He makes a close study of authors and their publishers in late-Victorian and Edwardian London, a time and place when both literary forms and publishing practices were in the process of dramatic transformation. McDonald introduces his readers to Pierre Bourdieu's cultural theory. For Bourdieu, the literary field is 'a social "microcosm" that has its own "structure" and its own "laws"; while writers, critics, and, indeed, publishers, printers, distributors, and readers are "specialists" with "particular interests" specific to that self-contained world.'[18] McDonald applies this theory to the old flat communication circuit, and (without attempting a graphic representation) tweaks, stretches, multiplies, and morphs it. The result is a remarkably useful way of thinking about how literary compositions become the physical and commercial artefacts we call books. McDonald argues: 'Given that texts are radically situated, for Bourdieu, as material forms with a specific status in the field, the first task of any literary analysis is not to interpret their meaning, but to reconstruct their predicament.'[19] That situation, commercial, cultural, intellectual, and transitory, is only partially mapped by Darnton's communication circuit; the primary task is to reconstruct the literary field.

For Adams and Barker the life of a book is shaped by events, the first of which, publication, transforms it from the status of a manuscript to that of a book. For McDonald, interpreting Bourdieu, the Victorian literary text found itself in a predicament, that is, in a condition shaped by the design and format and marketing program applied to it by its publisher as well as its author. That text had been written by an author, but unlike Darnton's conceptualization of individualized, atomized authors and publishers, McDonald stresses the complexity of a literary culture. In turn-of-the-century London there were numerous groups and subgroups, many layers of status, numerous possible positions occupied by individuals in both categories. In three specific case studies he demonstrates how two competing approaches to literature – those of the 'purists' and those of the 'profiteers' – existed in tension with each other.[20] The writers and publishers of belles lettres and of other works for the discerning educated reader (of literary art for art's sake) disdained the work coming from the commercially oriented individuals and firms anxiously elbowing their way into an expanded and potentially lucrative market for popular fiction. And vice versa. Similarly an older generation, the established middle-aged writers and their heavyweight publishing counterparts, identified themselves as against the avant-garde upstarts. And again gender identities also set themselves in mutual opposition. The serious man of letters, writing for his intellectual peers, defined himself against the frivolous or over-emotional woman scribbler, who was catered to by those publishers who were prepared to offer her work to the distressingly undiscriminating masses.

Scholarship in book history has been peculiarly resistant to theory, and the antagonism of some literary historians to literary theory has hampered the application of cultural theory to the broader social networks among authors, readers and publishers. By invoking Bourdieu, McDonald brings to his meticulous reading of the empirical evidence about his three texts a welcome level of theoretical sophistication. The analysis concerns the value of identifying an author's or publisher's 'non-discursive position in the literary field,' that is, their socio-economic station apart from their location within the literary discourse. McDonald's acknowledgment of Darnton's contribution is generous and perceptive. He observes that the agents in Darnton's communication circuit are

> defined primarily in terms of their *function* in the process of *material* production. Authors produce manuscripts, publishers and distributors provide services, printers and binders supply skilled manual labour, and readers are end-product consumers. Given [Darnton's] particular goals, this basic functionalist insight into the workings of the entire circuit has obvious methodological value. The trouble is it brings blindnesses of its own. In particular, it fails to reckon on the other ways in which a literary culture is organized and, as a consequence, it writes out a further dimension to the overall process of production. First, the agents' positions in the culture are defined not only horizontally, in terms of their *function* in the circuit, but vertically, in terms of their *status* in the intricately structured field. Though these two dimensions are, of course, intimately related ... they are significantly distinct.

McDonald's work is highlighted here as a literary scholar's critique of Darnton, in that it shows up the latter's disciplinary assumptions about how books work. In a brief article about the application of Bourdieu's ideas to the history of the book McDonald observes trenchantly that Darnton is interested particularly in using book history as 'a way of re-thinking and re-writing non-book history.'[21] Similarly, McDonald is interested in using book history as a way of re-thinking and re-writing literary criticism, and it works.

James A. Secord: The Histories of the Book and of Science (2000)

Adrian Johns commented in 1994 on 'the simultaneous arrival over the last generation of both a new history of the book and a new history of science,' and suggested 'that a *rapprochement* might be highly beneficial to both camps.'[22] Such a rapprochement is now well underway, and one historian of science has addressed Darnton's model directly in the course of both using and contributing to the methods and theory of the history of the book. James A. Secord, whose earlier work was in the history of Victorian geology, turned his attention to nineteenth-century ideas about evolution in *Victorian Sensation: The Extraordinary Publication, Reception, and Secret Authorship of 'Vestiges of the Natural History of Creation.'* *Vestiges* was first published in 1844, and its anonymous authorship was part of the sensation it created, as was its discussion of evolutionary ideas about the natural world. This was fifteen years before Darwin's *On the Origin of Species* was published, and part of Secord's argument is to set the classic work in the context of its now-forgotten but then-sensational predecessor. As the subtitle of *Victorian Sensation* suggests, this is an account of the history of a single book, but Secord makes clear that his aim is not to write the 'biography' of a book, a description that is more appropriate for an account, such as Darnton's *Business of the Enlightenment* (1979), 'centred on production and authorship rather than reading.' Rather, Secord suggests:

> The remarkable story of *Vestiges* can be recovered through new approaches to reading and communication that are revolutionizing our interpretation of many aspects of the past. Reading has often been seen as a profoundly private experience, but it is better understood as comprehending all the diverse ways that books and other forms of printed works are appropriated and used. Taken in this sense, a history of reading

becomes a study of cultural formation in action. My strategy will be to follow a single work in all its uses and manifestations – in conversation, solitude, authorship, learned debate, religious controversy, civic politics, and the making of knowledge. We can then begin to understand the role of the printed word in forging new senses of identity in the industrial age. Rather unexpectedly, tracking a work like *Vestiges* proves to be especially revealing, for the handful of scientific books that become sensations have left more identifiable traces than comparable works of fiction, history, and poetry. References to fossil footprints and nebular Fire-mists have a specificity that makes their source relatively obvious. Because of this, a widely read scientific work is a good 'cultural tracer': it can be followed in a greater variety of circumstances than almost any other kind of book.

Secord characterizes his book as 'an experiment in a different kind of history,' one which takes reading seriously and uses reading practices to consider a 'major historical episode,' in this case the introduction of evolutionary thought.[23]

What the publication of *Vestiges* has to say about the 1840s, and also about the Darwinian moment of the 1850s, in Victorian culture is undeniably revealing. In Secord's words, 'every act of reading is an act of forgetting ... The books that allow us to forget the most are accorded the authority of the classic ... The *Origin* is among the most pervasive remnants of the Victorian world in our culture, yet it simultaneously forces much of that world into oblivion ... In remembering the *Origin* we forget *Vestiges*.'[24] And in reading *Vestiges* we forget the books that came before it.

Although few books are as suitable as *Vestiges* for this kind of study, Secord's contribution to the theory of studies of book and print culture is substantial. As we have seen, reading and readership studies have been largely, though not exclusively, concerned with reconstituting past encounters with novels and poetry; McDonald's work is an exemplary case in point. The problematic becomes quite different, however, when the issue is 'how can we understand this event, or that episode?' rather than 'how did contemporaries experience this author, or that canon?' Darnton's explorations into the history of the book and of reading in eighteenth-century France might be characterized as approaches to the question 'what made the French Revolution happen?' Similarly, Secord's questions about the way nature was understood in early Victorian England are historians' questions. In formulating answers he has drawn upon, and generously acknowledged, the work of bibliographers and book historians, and repays the debt by offering a new insight into how to theorize the way the book works in a given culture.

Secord introduces the notion of 'literary replication.' This metaphor replaces Darnton's image of circulation with one of replication. Like cells, texts replicate themselves, but with variants; and like organisms, books evolve from one state to the next. Copies of books are reproduced by the technology of the printing press, but to examine the sequence of editions is to discover that reproduction does not imply precise copying. On the contrary, the same title often appears over significantly different texts as well as widely diverging physical formats. Copies may be authorized by writer and publisher, or 'pirated' by others; readers may make copies for their own use; and a later generation's reading will differ from that of the author's contemporaries. Secord's critique of Darnton's model emphasizes that the language of circuitry puts too much stress on feedback and not enough on how books work outside the book trade in which they are made.

The notion of literary replication draws upon the extensive recent work in the history of science, where scholars now argue that the norms of modern science have been socially constructed.[25] Earlier scholarship had understood experimental replication as a merely mechanical process; new studies demonstrate that such replication is 'an accomplishment, achieved through agreement that two experiments are in fact "the same."' Secord suggests an analogy between conceptualizations of scientific experiment and of the authorship/printing/reading event. Like scientific replication, printing was formerly understood as merely mechanical; but research in the history of books has demonstrated that printing too is an 'accomplishment' wherein people associated with the book trades agree that one edition of a book is 'the same' as another. The reading public's conviction that one edition or reissue of a book is identical to and carries the same authority as another is an active accomplishment of the book trades. When successive editions and readings of *Vestiges* appeared in 1844 and throughout the 1850s, there was no single consensus over what the book meant, but instead a series of unstable and contingent agreements, especially fluid since Robert Chambers' authorial identity was hidden for so long.

The lesson Secord has taken from book history and bibliography is 'that textual stability, even within a single edition, has been difficult to achieve.' *Vestiges*, like other important books, was replicated throughout its contemporary culture – in numerous variant editions and in lengthy excerpts embedded within reviews and rebuttals. The printed text came to the attention of readers in the several places where each was ready and able to absorb it, and prepared to re-'publish' it, in conversation. The material replication of the printing shop (itself a cultural process) was part of the background to conversations about the book, in settings from the pub to the boudoir – and to lectures by authorities on both sides of the evolution question. And the cultural replication was framed, in its turn, by the printerly conventions of type and paper, design and marketing. Another way to put this would be to reflect on how book history is sometimes conceptualized as the study of authorship, reading, and publishing; by declining to give primacy to any of the three elements of the communication circuit Secord's analysis transcends them all. It is contextual in the fullest sense of the word, concerning the ways that books work in a culture, how they exercise their power.

The historians of science, like cultural historians and others working under the large umbrella of historical studies, have contributed a rich dimension to the history of books and print cultures. Significantly, their contribution is not stand-alone book history but is embedded in questions that matter intensely to scholarship in another discipline.[26] Just as Darnton asks about how reading contributed to the French Revolution,[27] Johns, Secord, and others have questions to ask about early modern and Victorian ideas of nature, and they find answers in the nature of the early modern and Victorian book trades and reading practice.[28] Might it be that scholarship like this, using the book as an intellectual approach and a way to open up interpretive possibilities, is even more fruitful than the sort of studies that focus inward upon the complexities of books for their own sake?

4

Where Is *the Book* in History?

In the material sense the book is of course everywhere in historical study, but *the book* in the sense of being a vehicle for thinking about the past is just coming into its own. As artefacts of the past books suffer among historians from the familiarity that breeds contempt. And as subjects of historical interest they may initially seem to belong within the scholarly preserves of bibliographers and literary scholars.

For many practitioners of history the book has not seemed to have a history at all, at least not in the strong sense of being engaged with agency. As an object the book may have a history in the sense that the steam engine or the corset has its own history, or that any surviving artefact of the past may be the subject of a chronological narrative that memorializes its origins and traces a line of development (or indeed decline) as its trajectory approaches the present day. But relatively few historians have yet become convinced that books have a history in the sense that Canada or capitalism has a history, or democracy or domesticity, or women or the working class. Literacy has a history; so does literature – but do books? That is, do the historian's fundamental questions apply to the printed-and-bound artefacts resting on library shelves? The discipline's questions are about change, about the causes and effects of political, economic, social, and cultural forces. The answers must be argued, not merely asserted, and those arguments are only beginning to be made. Recent scholarship, of which a sampling is reviewed here, suggests that the book may have been concealed as a potential subject of historical investigation behind the mask of its own ordinariness – the surface contemporaneity of a medium whose conventions have actually been radically transformed over centuries.

In locating the history and culture of the book within history per se, that is within a taxonomy of concerns of the whole historical discipline, a good place to start might be from the centrality of agency, and power, and experience, to use the formulation articulated by Judith Walkowitz. With these concepts in mind, it becomes quite clear that the historian construes the book in terms that have more to do with communication, knowledge, and culture than with either text or document/object. The abstract nature of this conceptualization requires a robust theoretical formulation. Robert Darnton, as we have seen, formulated the history of books in terms of a communication circuit and has continued to stress communication – more recently in the interactive website linked to his article in the *American Historical Review* in 2000. In that piece he argues that 'communication systems have always shaped events.'[1] Similarly in France the book remains of great interest to academic historians because of what it says about the dissemination of ideas and, more abstractly, of *mentalités*, or culture. *L'histoire du livre* emerged from the Annales school of historical research and practice, where the investigation of working-class reading material paralleled that of demographic and other trends in social history.[2] Anthony Grafton has observed that the Annales school, especially the work of Lucien Febvre, 'showed that one could trace, in precise detail, the ways that printing altered the lives of authors and readers, using the new, larger libraries of the age to chart transformations in the climate of opinion.' It is no coincidence that *L'Histoire de l'édition française* (1982–6) was the first of the national book-history projects. Its editors chose, as Roger Chartier explains, 'to consider the printed book as a commodity – an object produced by a specific technique and characterized by its own forms – as a new means of cultural communication.'[3]

If a commodity can be an agent of change, then Thomas R. Adams and Nicolas Barker's definition of the book in terms of a 'bibliographical document,' as 'something printed or written in multiple copies that its agent ... produces for public consumption,' now begs the question of agency. In other words, the bibliographers' core idea, that the material form of a text affects (and to some extent effects) the meaning attached to it by the recipient, brings the historian up against the question of who endows the object with its form, and the extent to which the perpetrator (or perpetrators) intend the meaning (or meanings) which the recipients perceive.

Like other aspects of cultural history, such as questions of labour or of gender, studies of the book by historians are centrally concerned with the problem of agency. And just as labour and gender studies must unpack popular notions of the revolutionary significance of such technologies as steam engines or oral contraceptives, scholarship in the history of books has to deal with the notion that the printing press was an agent of change. Elizabeth L. Eisenstein's magisterial 1979 work, for example, is entitled *The Printing Press As an Agent of Change: Communications and Cultural Transformations in Early-Modern Europe*. However, as Eisenstein herself accepts, the concept of technological determinism offers too simplistic an argument – whether exemplified by printing with movable types, or by later changes concerned with the mechanization of the book trades; the notion that mere technology shapes the impact of the book is compelling, but mistaken.

The history of the book has received a certain notoriety from Marshall McLuhan's linking of the medium with the message, a formulation that is strongly technologically determinist. Even before McLuhan, the political economist

Where Is *the Book* in History? 49

Harold Innis addressed, in *Empire and Communications* (1950), the problem of communication in historical terms. Peter Burke has described Innis's trajectory: 'The study of paper [as one staple industry in Canadian economic history] led him into the history of journalism, and the study of Canada, where communications mattered profoundly for economic and political development, colonial and postcolonial, drew him to the comparative history of empires and their media of communication, from ancient Assyria and Egypt to the present.' Innis was interested in how communication happens, and how to think about it. But he spoke of 'communication,' not 'the book,' when he invoked civilizations (such as Egypt) in which one small elite social group, perhaps a priesthood, held a monopoly on writing. Similarly he thought that in medieval Europe, 'the intellectual monopoly of medieval monks, based on parchment, was undermined by paper and print, just as the "monopoly power over writing" exercised by Egyptian priests in the age of hieroglyphs had been subverted by the Greeks and their alphabet.'[4]

Although Innis was an economist, not a historian, and did not use evidence in a way that was really satisfactory for historians, much of his theory was based upon an analysis of past cultures, of communication in past cultures. Not only did his imperial cultures go back to the beginning of writing, but he held an implicit theory that oral cultures were somehow more democratic, more humanistic, than writing-based cultures – and that only the latter could produce an empire. The theme of empire continues through the work – an empire is defined in terms of one culture's values being imposed upon another culture as 'an indication of the efficiency of communication.'[5]

McLuhan's work is much better known than that of Innis, whose influence he acknowledged. *The Gutenberg Galaxy* (1962) and *Understanding Media: The Extensions of Man* (1964) both discuss the cultural impact of the introduction of printing from movable type. Like Innis, McLuhan was fascinated with the way that print works: he said that print has an intrinsic bias, in that it has the power to separate readers from other forms of communication, not only from oral communication, but also from the visual arts. His famous aphorism that 'the medium is the message' (and later the 'massage') seems to sum up the argument of studies of book culture, and at the same time to trivialize it.

The thesis of *The Gutenberg Galaxy* is that the invention of printing with movable type has had a profound effect on events – not a single effect, but a whole galaxy or configuration of events. McLuhan introduced the powerful concept of 'print culture,' which 'suggested links between the new invention and the cultural changes of the period, without always specifying what these links might be.' When McLuhan said that the printing press meant the end of manuscript culture, he had not undertaken archival or bibliographical research into what has since developed into a rich vein of inquiry in medieval and Reformation/Renaissance studies. Rather, he was expressing his assumption, or hunch, that a dramatic break must have happened. As we shall see, that assumption is not valid, however compelling it may sound to the modernist.[6] He further argued that printing promoted nationalism, and national languages, and also fostered a sense of private identity (because individual readers had their own copies of printed books in hand).

For McLuhan, as for Innis, writing was a powerful technology, but printing was much more so. McLuhan had a dramatic impact on historical studies of printing and print culture, as the inspiration for Eisenstein's influential work. As Burke says, Eisenstein 'domesticated' the ideas of McLuhan (and of Walter Ong on orality) 'by translating them into terms which would be acceptable to her own professional community, that of historians and librarians.'[7] Adrian Johns refers to McLuhan as Eisenstein's 'inspiration and bête noire.'[8] Eisenstein has denied that her work implies a crass technological determinism, and has repeatedly taken pains to make her intentions and her argument clear.[9] But the implication that technology determines meaning by creating textual stability has been difficult to dislodge. Nevertheless, in the last twenty years the scholarship on reading and publishing in past cultures has convincingly demonstrated that the agency in question is human and social, not mechanical.[10] The significance of the new consensus, however, with its implication that print does not necessarily serve to fix a text, now or in the past – that print is only relatively less malleable and unstable a form than the computer screen or the copyist's script – is just beginning to be recognized. Once the agency associated with the object-book is located in the collective hands of its authors, compilers, editors, plagiarists, printers, and publishers, along with those of people in such related positions as bookseller, librarian, and reader-aloud, it is possible to consider the complex way in which books mediate between author and reader in the transmission of ideas. Or as Burke says: 'It might be more realistic to view print, like new media in later centuries (television, for example), as a catalyst, assisting social changes rather than originating them.'[11]

This kind of critique of the technological agency of printing has arisen not only directly in the history of communication but also indirectly, by way of the search for methodological innovation within the history of science. An issue of the *British Journal for the History of Science* in 2000 devotes a special section, 'Book History and the Sciences,' to articles working within the bibliographical conventions of book history, as an adjunct to the intellectual problems of history of science. In a brief 'Introduction' to that section Jonathan Topham remarks:

> Indeed, to the question 'what is book history for?' we might answer that its object is to reintroduce social actors engaged in a variety of practices with respect to material objects, into a history in which books have too often been understood merely as

disembodied texts, the meaning of which is defined by singular, uniquely creative authors, and as transparent to readers.[12]

One contributor to the section, Adrian Johns, has written extensively about this very issue. Briefly in a 1994 article, and in a full-length monograph, *The Nature of the Book*, in 1998, Johns has demonstrated that:

> Where work has been done, its concentration on fixity has tended to draw attention away from, rather than towards, the labour exerted by actors to keep their products stable across space and time. The effect has been still to privilege the work of certain individuals and institutions over others. A better way to proceed is to focus on just that very labour which such a treatment underplays.

Indeed, the correlation of printing with fixity of text 'is probably the most powerful force resisting the acceptance of a truly historical understanding of print and any cultural consequences it may foster.'[13] No consequential history of books and the cultures they inhabit will be possible until historians take mutability, not fixity, as their starting point.

In *The Nature of the Book* Johns demonstrates that the making of an authoritative text, in this case about natural knowledge, is a matter of historical problematic, rather than something to be taken for granted in the service of an argument about the revolutionary effect of printing on European ideas and culture. In the process he produces a splendid example for this section's exploration of historians' approaches to writing the history of the book.

Human agency is central to historians' characterizations of the book as a force in history, and although writers and readers have their places, the mediating agency of publishers is particularly relevant. (In earlier centuries the gatekeeper role of the publisher was held by stationers or booksellers or other agents of production and distribution.) Their importance has been characterized by Chartier: 'The publishing activity that chooses or orders texts, controls the operations by which texts become books, and assures their distribution among buyers is clearly the fundamental process where the interconnection occurs between the history of techniques and the history of production, the sociology of the book trade and the sociology of reading, the physical study of books, and the cultural study of texts.'[14]

The Problematic of Communication in Past Cultures

This section reduces the study of that history in which books have their part to the dimensions of time, place, and change over time, and uses these most basic of concepts to raise some questions about their application to the study of book and print cultures.[15]

Time

Within historical studies an ongoing concern is the problem of how to avoid being trapped in the arbitrary categories of periodization, the problem that Ludmilla Jordanova calls 'dividing up the past.' The periodization we still use was itself socially constructed within the community of academic historians, at about the same late-nineteenth-century point that history was reinvented as an academic discipline. The conventional periodization since then has been to divide the past into ancient, medieval, early modern, and modern periods, with further subdivisions within the main categories. Those periods are, of course, inherently Eurocentric. And indeed, we might ask how well they serve the cultural and social history even of Europe, where the useful term 'premodern' increasingly supersedes the strict break between medieval and early modern. In Ludmilla Jordanova's words, the 'inheritance' of earlier ideas about periodization is unfortunate, 'because conventionalised period terms seem to hamper fresh thinking; through periodisation particular views of history are naturalised, so that it is difficult to bring them up for critical scrutiny.'[16]

Periodization within book history tends to follow, even to reinforce, the conventional splits. In the orthodox textbook narrative, as we have seen, Gutenberg and the beginning of printing with movable types is often seen as one of the most important markers of the break between medieval and modern, manuscript and oral culture on the one hand and print on the other. It is worth noting that there is a certain slippage between setting up the contrast as manuscript/print, which focuses on the book, or orality/literacy, which focuses on the social context. There is a chronological parallel between illiteracy and orality on the part of ordinary people in the pre-industrial past on the one hand, and the circulation of books in manuscript form during the same centuries on the other. But manuscript culture was literate, and the relationship between literacy and the circulation of printed materials remains an open historiographical question.

The tight connection between print and modernity is particularly strong when technology drives the argument; studies of the history of printing and publishing usually develop a periodization extending from the mid-fifteenth century until the 1820s. It is well known that there was little change in the press or other printing trades for nearly four centuries, until stereotype plates were introduced, along with machine printing and machine-made paper.[17] *L'Histoire de l'édition française* characterizes this long period as 'a typographical *ancien régime*,' a periodization which itself cuts across the conventional rupture created by the French Revolution.[18]

However, if the history of the book, of communication through the written word made public, is articulated differently, then the periodization will change. If the problematic is literacy rather than printing – a social technology rather than a mechanical one – then the key dates will be somewhat different. In an overview study of literacy in early modern Europe R.A. Houston observes: 'In the cities of northern Italy, a "literate mentality" was already present in the fifteenth century, but in the Russian empire verbal communication remained dominant until the nineteenth century.' Houston also makes the point that 'using literacy was a complex process.' Similarly David Vincent's study of literacy and popular culture digs deep into aspects of Victorian working-class culture and imagination to develop an argument about the diverse uses of literacy, where skills varied according to the perceived need to acquire and apply them.[19]

If literacy is a matter of culture, not of technology, then it is part of the history of reading. The first generation of *l'histoire du livre* in France did not ask the questions that now loom so large, about how reading might have changed over time; the assumption was that both text and reading, as abstractions, remained immutable. As Chartier observes, one of the drawbacks of his predecessors' having 'remained indifferent to the objects themselves' was that it prevented them from 'responding to one of the fundamental questions [book history] sought to address: that is to say, in what manner did the circulation of more and more printed texts modify thoughts and sensibilities?'[20] Chartier's own work has since done much to transform the problematic of reading in historical perspective, and other historians (as well as scholars in other disciplines) have contributed substantially to the literature. James Raven suggests: 'If we ... discard assumptions of simple polarity between literacy and non-literacy, we have to rethink our appraisal of reading as an aspect of cultural change in the eighteenth century.' Warning against the identification of reading in terms of 'improvement and enlightenment, of progress from lesser to greater literacy, from ignorance and barbarism to democracy, humanitarianism and virtue,' he argues that 'attempts to understand the historical individual reader might, above all, check Whiggish accounts of the purpose and effects of reading.'[21] The Whiggish, or presentist, assumptions – that reading was for improvement and its effects were modernizing – go hand in hand with similar assumptions about the technology of printing.

This distinction among the periodizations of technology, of literacy, and of reading is not meant to privilege one over the others, but rather to suggest that studies of book culture must be attentive to their own complex problems of periodization. As in other new cultural histories, intellectual curiosity, fuelled by political engagement, will freshly illuminate conventional aspects as well as propound a new set of questions. Perhaps an analogy will be helpful: one important early work in women's history (also an approach to a previously neglected aspect of the past) is an article by Joan Kelly-Gadol entitled 'Did Women Have a Renaissance?' in which she argues that they did not. The conventional periodization had proved unhelpful for women's history, in that the great dividing point of human history in the West, the rebirth of classical knowledge and so on, marked no positive change in the lives of women of any social class. Indeed, Kelly-Gadol suggests, the Renaissance was a significant date or event in women's history only in the negative sense of *reducing* options for women.[22]

Similarly, book historians need to be conscious of the significant periodization for book-trade events: scholars who work in the fifteenth, sixteenth, and seventeenth centuries might well question the easy allocation of 1450 as a 'rupture' or 'shift' in the history of the book, and remember that for scholars who work in premodern studies the adoption of the codex was more significant than the beginning of printing. Chartier revises the stress laid by Henri-Jean Martin on the importance of Gutenberg and his technology: 'Printing ... does not constitute,' in his opinion, 'the same sort of rupture as that which occurred during the second and third centuries A.D.,' when the *volumen*, or scroll, was replaced by the *codex*, and parchment was largely superseded by paper.[23] And as we have seen, the long survival of a typographical ancien regime did not preclude profound changes in other aspects of bookish culture, not only in the trade itself, but with the habits of mind associated with literacy and reading.

Place

Historians of the book trade have been richly rewarded by attending closely to its geography, as did Lucien Febvre and Henri-Jean Martin, whose collaborative work *The Coming of the Book* is a founding text of the field.[25] Both Peter W.M. Blayney and Raven have mapped the bookselling districts of London in their respective periods, and Fiona Black and Bertrum H. MacDonald have suggested how the use of new technologies of mapping can open up new questions. Geographic Information Systems (GIS) may be used 'to move from examining a relatively static "geography" of book production to investigating the dynamic "spatial history" of the multifaceted concept of print culture, by relating information about books and their production, dissemination, and reception to a potentially wide range of spatially related historical information.'[24]

As we move from the temporal dimension to the geographical, we might use Kelly-Gadol's transformative question as a model: 'Did books have national boundaries?' That is, should the nation-state, itself a rather modern concept, be the appropriate framework within which to construct cohesive histories of the book in all its forms – including the medieval manuscripts of a unified Catholic Europe and the websites of the twenty-first century global village, not to mention the carved stone of the ancient world or the wampums of certain North American native peoples? Put that way, it is plain that national boundaries are an artificial and limiting notion, before one even considers the ease with which the book trades have always made shipments, legitimate and otherwise, from the place of origin to the book's destination in a reader's hands. But even if we can agree that books as media of communication were not limited by national boundaries in the past, we cannot ignore the nation state. As it happens, national histories do seem to be seriously bound up with books.

Benedict Anderson has argued that nations can be seen as 'imagined communities.' This powerful conceptualization, which has influenced numerous historians and social and political thinkers over the past several years, is largely based on characterizing national identity in terms of reading. People who read the same text, whether a newspaper or a novel, especially if they read it at about the same time, are in a sense constituting themselves as a community, although they are unknown to each other as individuals. For Anderson, 'the book was the first modern-style mass-produced industrial commodity.' Unlike agricultural or craft commodities, however, 'the book ... is a distinct, self-contained object, exactly reproduced on a large scale.' From this perspective the newspaper is merely 'a book sold on a colossal scale, but of ephemeral popularity. Might we say: one-day best-sellers?' Reading, especially newspaper reading, can be construed as a kind of communion, or moment of common prayer: 'It is performed in silent privacy, in the lair of the skull. Yet each communicant is well aware that the ceremony he performs is being replicated simultaneously by thousands (or millions) of others of whose existence he is confident, yet of whose identity he has not the slightest notion.' Thus for Anderson, the book trade is a 'silent bazaar' that links producers with consumers of writings that invoke national identity. Anderson has observed that 'the convergence of capitalism and print technology on the fatal diversity of human language created the possibility of a new form of imagined community, which in its basic morphology set the stage for the modern nation.'[25] If the very concepts of nation and of national identity are historically situated, contingent on events, then equally so are the concepts of text, book, and document.

The historiographical parallels are suggestive. While political-constitutional history is often specific to the nation state, cultural history – or social or family or gender history – is often usefully studied in a broader geographical compass. If 'childhood' or 'literacy' or 'women' can be studied across national boundaries, it is worth asking why 'the book' – an eminently transportable proposition, whether considered as text or object – is so often tightly framed in terms of national identity. D.F. McKenzie has suggested the possibilities of a comparative history: 'national histories which take the *book* as their subject have at base a common artefact, using comparable means of production and distribution to serve comparable ends.'[26] Why, then, are we so prone to study each nation's book trade in isolation?[27] This is not the place for a full discussion of answers to that question, but one possibility might be suggested. This is the accident of the first 'national book-history project' emerging in France, a country whose specificity as a nation-state with a compelling, indeed revolutionary, history has shaped its historiography in particular ways. Chartier's article 'Frenchness in the History of the Book' traces that historiography from the 1950s to the present day, linking each trend in *l'histoire du livre* with trends in broader historical practice, first a quantitative enthusiasm, then an overwhelming primacy attached to social class, or in his words, 'economic and social [history] based on numbers and series ... [and] the kingdom's administrative and notarial archives.'[28] These later gave way to a concentration on cultural forms, including a new appreciation for the book as material object. This inward focus – it was Darnton who called it 'Frenchness' – along with the evolution of the Annales tradition, explains why so much energy was put into creating a brilliant *Histoire de l'édition française* (1983–6), and also suggests why the histories of other nations' books may look rather different.

Over the past dozen years projected histories of the book in Britain (but also Scotland, Wales, and Ireland), in Australia, New Zealand, Germany, the United States, Canada, and other places have begun to fall into line behind the

French model. But now that these works are beginning to appear, and conversations between and among the various projects have occurred, a new question is being formulated: do the book-trade similarities from one nation to another perhaps outweigh their national differences? Within the trade we can certainly identify some common themes for western cultures. The conference 'Worldwide Changes in Book Publishing from the Eighteenth Century to the Year 2000,' held in Sherbrooke, Québec, was illuminating in this regard. The history of the book in the modern world was presented by an international body of scholars, first country by country, and then genre by genre.[29] One common theme that emerged in discussion was the relationship of centre and periphery. Within the boundaries of a single nation it is the tension between a metropolis like Paris or London (or New York or Toronto) and other places where the literati are less likely to gather, but whose own kind of political and social power can nevertheless affect the culture of the metropolis. We have often read about how even books as closely associated with a country and its culture as, for example, the novels of Dickens with Victorian England were disseminated (and appropriated) globally, across the boundaries of nation-state and of national language; similarly in the context of empire, books are one of the communication media used to create and maintain control, or at least to attempt such control.

Despite the permeability of political borders nation is not irrelevant in the history of the book. But it is problematic. If theoretical and methodological problems are considered, then we are back in the realm of difference. One example might be the question of when and where in Canadian history to begin the narrative. The editors of *A History of the Book in Canada* opted for the initial encounter of native people with printing, and also show how even among European settlers the question of a starting point is complex; books were imported from Paris, London, and elsewhere long before printing began in the colonies. New

France also supported a rich scribal tradition, as François Melançon's work suggests.[30] As Germaine Warkentin observes, 'the presence of nearly two hundred years of scribal culture thus makes print seem less the culminating achievement and dominant motif of Canadian book history than a specific, and historically delimited, episode in our cultural narrative.' Moreover (as Warkentin also demonstrates) there was also a system of written communication, used by native Canadians, based upon signification systems such as wampums; it was a semasiographic or pictographic sign system, rather than one that was based on language, or phonographic, and it was essentially 'bookish.'[31] My point in this brief digression is to show that the questions of what to include within, and exclude from, a history of communication will differ not only from time to time but from place to place. The differences will be dictated not so much by the application of the technologies and practices of the book trade, here or there, but by the theoretical assumptions, whether stated or not, of the scholars who are marking out the limits of both *book* and *history*.

Change over Time

Most historical studies have been concerned with the way that change happened within past cultures. If we identify some of the conventional notions about forces of change within larger societies, such as secularization, industrialization, political ideologies, and demographic transformations, it is obvious that these forces have affected the dynamics of authorship, the book trades, and reading habits within those societies. The key questions here are political and economic, and may first be phrased as 'where does the power lie?' States hold the power of censorship; both absolutist royal regimes and the command economies of the former Soviet Union have exercised censorship as a tool of power. And even in professedly liberal societies the social power of institutions, such as churches and universities, can be profound. So can the cultural power of ideologies. Darnton writes about the libertine literature that was part of the culture of dissent in *The Forbidden Best-Sellers of Pre-Revolutionary France*. Another example comes from the informal censorship imposed on Victorian publishers in Britain by the conventions valued by the circulating libraries.[32]

The book trade is intrinsically commercial, and hence its history is bound up in changes from precapitalist to capitalist systems, and in some places with experience in communist or other alternatives. The notion that publishing is both cultural and commercial, that the book is a commodity as well as a work of literary art, has underpinned scholarly understanding for many years.[33] Raven has argued that 'all national models of the book trades in early modern and modern Europe are variants of one European model dominated by issues of capitalization, central control, centralised production and radial distribution networks.'[34] One way in which to recognize the commercial nature of the book trade is to reflect upon how exceptional are the occasions when print is circulated at no charge to the reader, as do the contributors to *Free Print and Non-commercial Publishing since 1700*.[35]

How, then, does a historical problematic shape the formulation of a coherent theory and methodology for book history? One way to formulate those questions might be to remember that the conventional book history categories of authorship, reading, and publishing are chronologically and geographically contingent, specific to the modern period and to western cultures. They are also inevitably slanted towards literary works. In the interests of interdisciplinary and transnational approaches it might be helpful to make those categories less bound by assumptions of a particular time and place. Rather than authorship some scholars have focused on *composition* or *inscription*, so as to include transcriptive acts of writing, such as the recording of communal endeavours, or collective feats of memory like folk tales, songs, or recipes.[36] To historicize authorship is to contemplate how concepts of the value and ownership of literary property change over time. Laws of copyright are complex, and the specific conditions under which they are modified may be obscure, but such landmarks in literary history as the rise of the novel are directly related to the monetary rewards that were available to authors and their heirs.[37] Similarly, the terminology of a *production-distribution continuum* is preferable to making sharp distinctions between publishing and bookselling (both which took on their modern forms in the eighteenth century). To recognize that the publisher function was once carried out by stationers and booksellers is to become aware that retail bookselling is a neglected aspect of studies of book culture.[38] And instead of readership, *reception* is a term perhaps broad enough to embrace the possibility of using the book for purposes other than reading. Even though much of the most exciting new scholarship puts the reader in the foreground in relation to a book's composers, producers, and distributors, the perception that some works are designed to be consulted or collected, rather than consumed and shared, puts those relationships into perspective.[39]

These suggestions are not intended to diminish or dismiss the importance of the authorship, reading, and publishing of the creative literary work of the past two centuries. They are, rather, intended strongly to suggest that different approaches, methods, and research problematics can be applied to the histories of books of hours, bibles, cookbooks, chronicles, histories, political and philosophical treatises, government reports, conduct books, textbooks, scientific works, dictionaries and encyclopedias, and all the other manuscript, printed, and electronic texts that are lumped as non-fiction. The utility of the history of books is not limited to answering questions such as how the Victorians read Dickens: understanding how they read Mrs Beeton is a different matter, and one that 'leads out into social history' (in Darnton's words) in a different way.[40] In Matthew Brown's provocative words, 'book history challenges literary critics because its insights recover titles that are – as scholars of literary art see matters – substantively boring. What book-trades research, printhouse studies, sales records, readership histories, and every other page of *PABH* [*PBSA*] suggest is that information-based texts drive the production and consumption of written records. Discontinuous information, not fictional art or linear narratives. What will literary critics do with this point?' Yet surely, he muses, 'a history of consciousness, of affect and imagination, of politics and conflict, can be explored through this boring canon.'[41] Indeed it can. Historians, whose disciplinary practice is not construed around a canon, are unlikely to be either bored or disconcerted by the titles they encounter on the books produced and distributed in past cultures.

5

Cross-Disciplinary Observations: The Mutability of Texts, Print, and Readings

The discussion in chapter 4 of the impact of McLuhan's speculative ideas highlights the powerful theory that printing with movable types was revolutionary because it allowed the production and replication of a standardized, or fixed, version of a text in many copies. The juxtaposition of the Gutenberg moment with such historical developments as the Reformation, the Renaissance, and the Scientific Revolution has given rise to what Robbie McClintock calls a chicken-and-egg argument: which came first, and what caused what?[1]

Elizabeth Eisenstein's theory concerning the agency of the technology of printing is built on an argument that printing with movable types served to 'fix' the texts of important works of the Renaissance and the Reformation. For her the shift from script to print is 'the unacknowledged revolution' in Europe's history, and in chapters on religion, humanistic philosophy, and science she deploys the traditional non-bibliographical evidence of the intellectual historian to make the case for technological agency. She argues that it was printing – of scriptures (as well as tracts) in the vernacular languages of Europe – that served to make Luther's heresy a permanent reformation, rather than a local schism to be suppressed by Rome. In the case of science, or 'natural philosophy,' Eisenstein similarly argues that because the technology of printing served to fix the text of a scientific work, that discourse thereby took on its modern air of authority. Eisenstein's book received severe criticism from bibliographers and textual scholars at the time the original two-volume edition of her work appeared in 1979.[2] Nevertheless, many of the standard textbooks used in North American universities cite *The Printing Press as an Agent of Change* to help explain Luther's success.[3]

The implications of the Eisenstein case for historians and literary scholars – that bibliographical evidence not only can be useful but must be considered when dealing with the mechanisms of cultural transmission – have only recently been fully addressed. As James Raven remarks: 'Narrow concentration upon changes in printing technology and press production tempts assumptions about unchanging responses to texts.' Perhaps as a consequence, 'many historians of the physical book have surely undervalued the instability of its reception – the different response to subtly different printings, editions and bindings and the broader context of typographical presentation in the first centuries of print. For some readers … sensitivity to variant editions was accentuated, with sophisticated appreciation of the mutability of the text.'[4]

Eisenstein was not interested in the mutability of the text but rather in 'the shift from one kind of literate culture to another,' which was what she had in mind 'when referring to an "unacknowledged revolution."'[5] She decided to work out this idea from within both the constraints of her discipline, history, and the problematics with which it was engaged in the 1960s and 1970s. Restating her twenty-year-old argument in a Forum in the *American Historical Review* in 2002, she reminds readers that her work 'was not intended to be framed by either the history of the book or the history of reading. Instead [she] had in mind a broader, currently unfashionable, unit of study: Western Civilization (or "Western Christendom" – as it was known in the fifteenth century).' She was 'particularly curious about the way changes affecting the transmission of texts over the course of many generations impinged upon historical consciousness,' and notes trenchantly that 'current trends in book history have pointed away from such concerns.'[6] In the *AHR* article she engages particularly with Adrian Johns' critique of her work in *The Nature of the Book*, and the editors of the *AHR* provided Johns with the space for an article-length response and gave Eisenstein the last word in a 'Reply.' Johns, as we have seen, made his points about the unstable, contingent nature of print in terms of human agency rather than the agency of the technology. Eisenstein cleverly recasts his critique in the language of an American political group, the National Rifle Association: 'guns don't shoot people, people do' – and similarly (my paraphrase): 'print doesn't create change, printers do.' Johns in turn characterizes his own approach as 'something like "guns don't kill people, society kills people."'[7]

The Johns-Eisenstein debate is illuminating, and a good starting point for students of history, especially as they enter the scholarly space of studies in book and print culture. The debate is partly a disparity between academic generations, where Eisenstein's preference for the impact of the technology and its historiographical acknowledgment has given way to Johns' interest in the social construction of ideas about the natural world and the discourse of his historical actors.[8] In some ways they write past each other, neither engaging with the other's main premise: Johns even frames Eisenstein's critique of his own work as an idiosyncratic reading, an example of how 'readings exemplify the active power of the critic to frame meanings out of what is on the page – a power that is very much part of the world of the book but is not an emergent property of the press itself and hence has no clear place in Eisenstein's notion of print culture.'[9]

Histories of reading, like those by Johns and James Secord in the history of science in the seventeenth and nineteenth centuries respectively, and by Kevin Sharpe in the history of the politics of early modern England, have done a great deal to unsettle arguments about fixity.[10] Such histories include not only the evidence that readers have left behind in diaries and commonplace books, but also the evidence that printers have left behind in the multiplicity of variant versions of texts of what superficially purports to be the 'same' work. Sharpe's is a study of early modern English political history as understood through reading, using the voluminous notes, annotations, and diaries of William Drake, who experienced the Civil War mainly through literature. Sharpe provides a lengthy discussion of the debate over interpretations of seventeenth-century English history in the opening section, 'Learning to Read,' and insists that 'for the historian of the Renaissance to ignore the theoretical and historical questions about reading, as well as writing, texts is to be guilty of anachronism.'[11]

Bibliographical scholarship, too, insists upon the mutable and malleable nature of the printed word. David McKitterick's *Print, Manuscript and the Search for Order, 1450–1830* considers, in exquisite detail and with precise illustrations (both textual and visual), 'what is meant by printing' in the period he addresses. His aim is 'to demonstrate that instability in print is not just a linear process, from speech to manuscript to print, nor even one that depends on the author at work among several parallel versions, none of which may be necessarily more or less authoritative in the sense that it was accepted by the author himself. The pedigree of this condition of instability may be traced back to the nature of the changes in procedures and methods of book production in the mid-fifteenth century. Instability is characteristic of each stage in the production of a book even after it has left the author's hands.' McKitterick speaks of the 'maverick quality' of the printed book, 'familiar to critical theory in literature and art alike, [which] challenges assumptions that books possess a uniformity not just of content, but even of interpretation.' Indeed, 'the most arresting quality of the printed word and image is that they are simultaneously fixed, and yet endlessly mobile.'[12] In stark contrast to Eisenstein's objection 'to quibbling over the fact that early copies were *not* all precisely alike,'[13] McKitterick says: 'A detailed reading of the catalogue of fifteenth-century printed books in the British Library ... makes plain something of the extent to which different copies in an edition varied amongst themselves, not just in decoration but also at the earlier stage, in settings of their texts and the typographical contexts presented by each page.'[14] Textual variance is more important than a quibble, but its importance is not easily reduced to textbook certainties about revolutionary change.

McKitterick also notes the way in which the instability of early-modern printed works could be, and was, concealed by their makers. Concluding a discussion of the role of the press corrector, he argues: 'The process of printing ... insisted on, and was defined by, a series of texts none of which could be regarded as stable. Despite claims otherwise, the process of printing was inherently unstable, not only in the well-documented habits of correction during press-runs but also in every stage that preceded them. The stability of the final published text depended on a visual sleight of hand in which most of the slippery manufacture was concealed.' Even the reader was 'responsible for a part of the book's physical manufacture' in this period: 'from the sixteenth to the eighteenth centuries, readers were requested by authors, stationers and printers alike to amend with the pen what had been set and printed in type.' However, McKitterick draws the line at much of the recent scholarship in the history of reading. The difficulty is 'that the reader takes command.' McKitterick has no more patience than Eisenstein with the argument that science is socially constructed, but he does seem to agree with Johns that because print was unstable 'readers' interpretations remained governable only to a very limited extent.'[15]

Like historians and bibliographers, literary scholars are stressing the mutability of the material text, as well as an author's intentions and a reader's interpretations. The preparation by a textual editor of a literary text for a new edition is an occasion for engagement with these problems. As we have seen, some of the earliest bibliographical scholarship came into being to solve the textual problems of deciding the authorial intentions of Shakespeare and of the first generation of American authors, and to prepare authoritative critical editions.[16] More recent editorial theory has abandoned the notion of establishing a single authoritative text. Paul Eggert offers a useful rationale for modern editorial practice:

> Editing ... privileges the agent and the moment of writing, and documents the writing process, Or, rather, it has the capacity to document the process; but its habit hitherto of constructing a single reading text and providing an apparatus to serve *it* has catered to the illusion that imaginative activity gives rise in almost every case to a stable textual product. This has in turn fuelled, by failing to challenge, the post-structuralist tendency to marginalize the author in order to give a free rein to the multiplicities of textuality and reconstitution. Editing procedures have tended to cast into the background the knowledge that literary works are not fixed but are, rather, unstable and problematic from the very start.[17]

Similarly, Leah S. Marcus in *Unediting the Renaissance: Shakespeare, Marlowe, Milton* engages with 'the variability over time and space of any given work ... The approach and critical interests we wish to bring to a given piece of writing may be facilitated, discouraged, or even blocked altogether by the specific version in which we receive it.'[18] Just as an earlier generation of critics depended upon the bibliographical certainties of Alfred Pollard, W.W. Greg, and Fredson Bowers, Marcus and others including Jerome McGann now base their work upon the more flexible bibliographical approach of D.F. McKenzie.

Marcus identifies a generational shift in textual studies:

when she was a graduate student of English in the late 1960s, 'most students avoided the bibliography courses like a plague: to specialize in such mechanical matters, we felt in what then passed for wisdom, was to give evidence of some grave defect of personality or imagination.' But since the late 1990s, at Texas, Emory, Toronto, Oxford, Cambridge, the University of California, and elsewhere, 'graduate students in literature are beginning to display what to an older generation of scholars is an almost heretical interest in physical objects from the past – early printed editions of the "classics," printed histories, chapbooks and popular literature of all kinds, manuscripts, manuscript books, and other artefacts ... these students find the problems of editing and classifying texts as captivating as other forms of interpretation.'[19] This generational difference, as we have seen, also applies in the discipline of history, where the socially constructed nature of cultural forms has drawn the interest of scholars like Johns and Secord.

Scholars in the mid-twentieth century found the idea of textual instability 'profoundly disquieting,' Marcus suggests, so that perhaps 'one of the functions of the standard edition was to calm that unease and convince readers that they were being offered a text that could be counted on.' But she finds that their granddaughters and grandsons, raised on television and conversant with the internet, feel no such unease: on the contrary, they are 'inclined to distrust editions that legislate a single set of meanings when their own sense of textual reality is multiple and protean. For them, instability does not necessarily provoke anxiety, but may be associated *à la* Barthes with feelings of play and release, or even with comfortable familiarity. These students are eager to work with primary materials ... instead of accepting received wisdom, particularly when that wisdom fails to confirm their own sense of the malleability of all discursive forms.'[20]

Johns the historian (of science), McKitterick the bibliographer, and Marcus the textual editor may be taken as exemplars of our three core disciplines and their work as demonstrations of their shared acceptance of the malleability of texts. They also exemplify the way in which the literature of studies in book and print culture draws upon, and engages in debate with, adjacent disciplines.

Discipline and Interdisciplinarity in Studies of Book and Print Culture

This essay has suggested that the primary disciplines in competition for 'ownership' of the book in past times are history, bibliography, and literary scholarship. They are by no means exclusive; other disciplines (such as communications studies, geography, political science, and sociology) and interdisciplinarities (cultural, classical, and medieval studies, women's studies, American, British, Canadian, and a whole alphabet of 'area studies') may be mapped onto these three core approaches, and each in turn divides into narrower fields. The practitioners of each pose different questions to the past, and indeed understand both *history* and *books* in different terms. And some pose their questions to the present, interrogating contemporary patterns of reception, production/distribution, and composition, while perhaps contemplating the future as well.

Moreover, as we have seen, the subject is of interest both to rigorous empiricists and to abstract theorists. This distinction cuts across formal disciplines, and it means that few assumptions are shared. Some practitioners, for example, do not challenge the notion that print has served to fix a text, thus ensuring that many readers experience the same words, on the same page, whereas others have foresworn the concept of fixity, and regard printed texts as only a little less fluid than manuscripts or electronic documents. Riotous interdisciplinarity indeed.

It is not really clear from Robert Darnton's article 'What Is the History of Books?' and its accompanying diagram how it is that the schematic model of the life-cycle of a book will help to alleviate disciplinary chaos. In this essay, however, I have problematized the boundaries and tensions between and among those scholarly disciplines that take an interest in the book in historical context. Three questions have been in the background throughout: Is book history even possible? Is book history actually history at all? And what is the history of the book for?

David Perkins' *Is Literary History Possible?* (1992) poses a teasing question that is appropriate for adaptation and reflection by historians of the book and students of book culture. Perkins answers his own question in the negative, concluding that literary history is not really possible to write in a way that is plausible. To be plausible the history of a literature would have to represent that literature's past existence, and at the same time explain its genesis and influence. He asks not whether literary history can be written, since it so voluminously is, but rather 'whether the discipline can be intellectually respectable,' and answers that 'we cannot write literary history with intellectual conviction, but we must read it.' Paradoxically, in Perkins' view, literary history is necessary, despite being impossible. He adds: 'The irony and paradox of this argument are themselves typical of our present moment in history.'[21]

To paraphrase Perkins' question, then: is book history possible? Will it repay the devotion of massive intellectual (and economic) resources? Inherent limitations, similar to those for literary history, include the difficulties of capturing the book's materiality in a past culture and simultaneously explaining where it came from and how its influence worked. Further limitations may be located in the disciplinary boundaries discussed above, the divergent, sometimes conflicting, approaches of scholars with different questions to ask. Does the study of book and print culture provide insights that can be discerned in no other way?

As we have seen, Perkins insists that literary history differs from history per se in that it 'is also literary criticism.

Its aim is not merely to reconstruct and understand the past, for it has a further end, which is to illuminate literary works.'[22] In a similar way the historian's brand of book history stands apart, and should stand apart, from both literary criticism and studies of the material book, in that its aim is to illuminate past cultures by revealing and analysing some of the ways in which literary, informational, ideological, and other works were composed, circulated, and received in those cultures.

Perkins' iconoclastic work suggests the second question, asking whether 'book history' is properly history at all, in the sense understood by members of professional academic historical institutions. While this essay has answered that question in the affirmative, it has also suggested why so few of its practitioners are to be found in university departments of history – matters of communication are only one among many problematics of concern to the discipline. And historians need to be convinced, not merely informed, of the utility of the bibliographical approach. The discipline recognizes book history *as* history when it offers a substantial body of evidence providing insights into the actions of men and women in the past, into their *mentalités* and ways of seeing, their struggles over power, their experience of the rhythms of life. To invoke the untranslatable language of *mentalités* with reference to the problematic of cultural history is to remember that the French historians who gave *l'histoire du livre* its (equally untranslatable) name were part of the Annales school, whose original members were preoccupied with what has been called, in another context, 'the informal logic of actual life,' that is, with culture.[23]

A third question almost as devastating as Perkins' has been posed by Johns: 'what is the history of the book for?' Johns answers in terms not of literature or of artefact, and not even of communication, but rather of knowledge: 'A plausible answer lies in the role played by written and printed materials in the constitution of knowledge. The history of the book is consequential because it addresses the conditions in which knowledge has been made and utilized. All of its further implications may be derived from this.'[24] The practices of printers and booksellers and the strategies of readers, in particular places at specific times, constitute those conditions.

To ask questions like these is to unsettle the complacency that exists alongside the recent burst of intellectual interest in the subject in academic circles. A similar critique comes from Sharpe, in *Reading Revolutions,* about the fragmentation inherent in an interdisciplinary field of study:

> The history of the book recognises that certain types of historical enquiry, the way in which questions are asked as well as answered, needs to be an interdisciplinary endeavour. And this, alas, is the problem as well as the promise of the history of the book. With some notable exceptions, there is always the danger that the history of the book fragments back into the smaller identity groups from which it was created. Traditional bibliographers and librarians do not always feel at home with sociologists and Annaliste historians, let alone critical theorists. Significantly this new discipline has done little to incorporate reception theory into a historical and material study of books and their readers. Moreover there is an equal danger that the history of the book is itself becoming a specialism, with its own conferences, journals and programmes (if not departments) – and a specialism that other 'mainstream' historians feel no guilt about ignoring or marginalizing.

Sharpe, like Johns, argues that the history of reading may be central to the understanding of the 'master narratives' of society and politics. [25]

If the history of reading is essential, and if we must understand the role of printers and writers and the materials they produced (and produce) in the constitution of knowledge, then how should such a broad subject be taught in the modern academy? Darnton's point about the complexities of interdisciplinarity still holds true, even if his model gives way to ungraphable concepts of replication and contingency. Given that the three core disciplines and the several related disciplines are profoundly institutionalized in universities and in the infrastructure of academia, we need to ask whether, and how, book history should also be institutionalized. Is book history to become a separate subject, like art history and the history of science, with a separate academic infrastructure of department, journal, and conference circuit, and its own theoretical and methodological discourse? Or alternatively, should the study of book cultures – present as well as past – be conceptualized institutionally in terms of a looser amalgam of disciplines and departments, as a program like women's studies, Renaissance, Victorian, or medieval studies, Canadian, American, Irish, or New Zealand studies, or gender and labour studies? Will its advanced students be able to secure academic appointments if their studies are not rooted in the disciplines in which they aspire to be appointed?

The special-interest courses, the degree programs, the periodicals, and the monograph series are immensely valuable in that they help to 'frame' the subject, to introduce students to its pleasures, and to put colleagues in touch with each others' ideas. They are not so much the harbingers of a new discipline, however, as aids to a productive, creative, and respectful interdisciplinarity. Each of the core fields of study will no doubt continue to approach the book from its own intellectual perspective, asking its own scholarly questions. Within historical studies the book history approach remains one powerful way of conceptualizing cultural history. But it is not necessary for historians to wrestle with either bibliographers or literary scholars for disciplinary ownership of the book. As we have seen, recent work in the history of science shows how easy it can be to miss the evidence of transmuting texts and multiplying readerships if apparently unproblematic artefacts, books, are not subjected to a rigid scrutiny. Studies of the utility of publishers' records and of readers' responses – as ways into an understanding of the genesis of literary texts – now suggest the possibility of using those same approaches for analysing cultural change in other arenas.

'Readers need to stand somewhere before they pick up a book,' observes Peter Rabinowitz.[26] Before they pick up the study of book and print culture, readers and scholars ought to identify which disciplinary field they find themselves standing in, and be prepared to discuss differences across the academic fence with respect and forbearance. The concern expressed in this essay about an orientation to the disciplinary boundaries in the study of book and print culture has to do, not with what Darnton calls 'interdisciplinarity run riot,' but rather with Cyndia Clegg's characterization of 'an undisciplined discipline.' The book is D.F. McKenzie's 'common artefact,' shared by many cultures, and its trade is Benedict Anderson's 'silent bazaar' where encounters both commercial and cultural occur. Students of the book are learning from our early experience the limitations of focusing inward, whether on the literary text, the material object, or even the apparently contextual theme of print culture. Each of these subjects of study, absorbing in itself, impinges on the other, and also upon broader contexts, of society, gender, and politics, and upon economic and intellectual factors.

Notes

Chapter 1 Disciplinary Boundaries and Interdisciplinary Opportunities

1 Readers who are interested in further information about developments and activities in studies in book and print culture are encouraged to investigate the activities of the international Society for the History of Authorship, Reading and Publishing (SHARP), whose website is www.sharpweb.org. A *Book History Reader* has been edited by David Finkelstein and Alistair McCleery (2002), who have also written *Introduction to Book History* (2005). The website 'Book History Online' can be found at www.kb.nl/bho.
2 Rabinowitz, *Before Reading*, 2.
3 For the association between the historian's history of the book and cultural transaction see Leslie Howsam, 'Book History Unbound.'
4 Thompson, *The Making of the English Working Class*, 9–11.
5 Michele Moylan and Lane Stiles, eds, *Reading Books*, 3.
6 Jonathan Rose, 'The Horizon of a New Discipline.'
7 Clegg, 'History of the Book,' 223.
8 Darnton, 'What Is the History of Books?' in *The Kiss of Lamourette*, 108.
9 For the punning title see Johns, *The Nature of the Book*. For fixity see also Johns, 'AHR Forum: How to Acknowledge a Revolution,' 106–25, discussed below.

80 Notes to pages 7–11

10 Barthes, 'The Death of the Author,' in *Image – Music – Text*, trans. and ed. Stephen Heath (London: Fontana, 1977), 142–8. Foucault, 'What Is an Author?' in *Language, Counter-Memory Practice: Selected Essays and Interviews*, ed. Donald Bouchard, trans. Donald Bouchard and Sherry Simon (Ithaca, NY: Cornell University Press, 1977), 133–8. For a comment on these two authors *as* authors see Juliet Gardiner, 'Recuperating the Author,' 255–74.
11 The full text of the BOOK joke is easily accessible, usually without attribution, on the internet. It seems to have originated before the advent of computing, with R.J. Heathorn, 'Learn with Book,' *Punch* (9 May 1962); reprt. in Phillip J. Hills, ed., *The Future of the Printed Word* (London: Greenwood Press, 1980), 171–2.
12 McKenzie, 'The Sociology of a Text: Orality, Literacy and Print in Early New Zealand,' 334.
13 Darnton, 'What Is the History of Books?' in *The Kiss of Lamourette*, 110; Sutherland, 'Publishing History: A Hole at the Center of Literary Sociology,' 576; Moylan and Stiles, eds, *Reading Books*, 3; Clegg, 'History of the Book,' 237. The following extract from Moylan and Stiles' introduction is helpful: 'The history of the book, as it has been practiced in the past and as it is now being practiced, involves not just cultural history but also material and economic history, bibliography and textual criticism, amateur antiquarianism, and archival compilation. If book history is to remain vital in the future, it must continue to incorporate and profit from this full range of scholarly activities. Most especially book historians must address the material book, as well as its cultural work, and explore the book trade as an economic and social, as well as a cultural, institution. The book, as physical artifact, acts finally as the touchstone with which we must test our abstract cultural insights and theories as we decide whether their gold is genuine or base' (viii).
14 McGann, 'Visible and Invisible Books,' 147.
15 For comments on the reluctance of historians to engage with the literary concept of 'new historicism' see David Allan,

'Some Methods and Problems in the History of Reading.' See also Hayden White's 'New Historicism: A Comment,' in H. Aram Veeser, ed., *The New Historicism* (New York: Routledge, 1989): 'The ways in which [New Historicists] construe the nature of the historical context give offense to historians in general. For the New Historicists, the historical context is the "cultural system." Social institutions and practices, including politics, are construed as functions of this system, rather than the reverse. Thus, New Historicism appears to be based on what might be called the "culturalist fallacy," which marks it as a brand of historical idealism' (294).

16 Greetham's *Theories of the Text* is important for students of any of the book-history disciplines who wish to understand how these disciplines relate to each other with respect to textual studies and textual editing. His introduction states: 'My theories of text are thus theories of writing and of reading, theories of intention and of reception, theories of transmission and of corruption, and theories of originary conception and of social consumption and variation. And my book is also an account of the dialogics, pluralities, and contradictions that these multiple processes engender – not one theory but many *theories of the text*' (1).

17 Jordanova, *History in Practice*, 58.

18 Walkowitz, *City of Dreadful Delight: Narratives of Sexual Danger in Late Victorian London* (Chicago: University of Chicago Press, 1992), 8.

19 Jordanova, *History in Practice*, 41–2. The biography of a book, or 'biblio-biography,' may, however, be to strain the metaphor too far. James A. Secord has stressed that books 'do not have a "life" of their own independent from their use': *Victorian Sensation*, 2.

20 Raven, *London Booksellers and American Customers*, xviii. Secord, *Victorian Sensation*, 518.

21 For an introduction see Philip Gaskell, *A New Introduction to Bibliography*. See also G. Thomas Tanselle, *Literature and Artifacts*.

22 Leslie Howsam, 'An Experiment with Science for the Nineteenth-Century Book Trade,' 202.

23 Adams and Barker, 'A New Model for the Study of the Book,' 13.
24 McKenzie, *Bibliography and the Sociology of Texts* (1986), 19–20.

Chapter 2   Mapping the Interdisciplinarities

1 Jordanova, *History in Practice*, 85.
2 Casper, *Constructing American Lives*, 15.
3 Perkins, *Is Literary History Possible?* 177.
4 Ezell, *Writing Women's Literary History*, 54.
5 Nicolas Barker has remarked: 'When people talk of "print culture" I wish I had a revolver to reach for' ('In Praise of Manuscripts,' in *Form and Meaning in the History of the Book*, 27). More temperately Joseph Dane has engaged critically with the concept from the standpoint of bibliographical and editorial practice in *The Myth of Print Culture*.
6 James P. Danky and Wayne A. Wiegand, eds, *Print Culture in a Diverse America*.
7 Rose, *The Intellectual History of the British Working Classes*; the book begins with 'A Preface to the History of Audiences' (1–11). For working-class readers see also David Vincent, *Bread, Knowledge and Freedom;* and R.K. Webb, *The British Working-Class Reader 1790–1848*.
8 McGill, *American Literature and the Culture of Reprinting*, 1, 2.
9 For reading groups see Juliet Gardiner, 'Recuperating the Author'; and Danielle Fuller and DeNel R. Sedo, 'A Reading Spectacle for the Nation.'
10 For reception theory see Wolfgang Iser, *The Act of Reading*; Iser, *The Implied Reader*; and Hans Robert Jauss, *Towards an Aesthetic of Reception*.
11 Allan, 'Some Methods and Problems in the History of Reading,' 104; Susan K. Suleiman and Inge Crossman, eds, *The Reader in the Text*; see also Stanley Fish, *Is There a Text in This Class?*
12 Stoddard, 'Morphology and the Book from an American Perspective,' 4.
13 Ronald B. McKerrow, *An Introduction to Bibliography for Literary Students*; Philip Gaskell, *A New Introduction to Bibliography*.

14 McKenzie, 'Sociology of a Text,' 335. McKenzie's use of the term 'sociology' in his Panizzi lectures (*Bibliography and the Sociology of Texts*, 1985) was specific and historical. He linked the career of Anthony Panizzi, the nineteenth-century librarian of the British Museum, to the etymology of the term coined by August Comte and made respectable by Herbert Spencer in *The Study of Sociology* (1873). My reading of McKenzie's use of the term is that he wished to avoid using 'social history' in this context because his remarks had a contemporary as well as a historical aspect. Academic sociologists have not, to my knowledge, commented on the concept of a sociology of texts from the perspective of their own discipline and its contemporary preoccupations, and they may well judge the term to be problematic.
15 McKenzie, *Bibliography and the Sociology of Texts* (1985), 6.
16 Moylan and Styles, eds, *Reading Books*, 2, 4. Moylan's own contribution to this volume is particularly interesting. She argues that 'we can look at textual materiality as one expression of ... an interpretive performance' ('Materiality as Performance: The Forming of Helen Hunt Jackson's *Ramona*,' in Moylan and Styles, eds, *Reading Books*, 224).
17 McGann, *The Textual Condition*; Shillingsburg, *Pegasus in Harness*.
18 Allan, 'Some Methods and Problems in the History of Reading,' 118, 117.
19 Jackson, *Marginalia*, 8, 15. See also Jackson, *Romantic Readers*; and Anthony Grafton, 'Is the History of Reading a Marginal Enterprise?' 139–57. Grafton argues that marginal annotations and excerpts copied into notebooks do what the best historical evidence always does: 'they give off the scent of human flesh and blood.' We learn that 'the Humanist turned to his books not only for information they could offer him, but also because they were his best confidants, the sharers of his most intimate thoughts – even if the conversation had to take place on paper and in an ancient language. Only the history of the books can enable us to eavesdrop on close encounters of this now-forgotten kind.'

20 St Clair, *The Reading Nation in the Romantic Period*, 42.
21 Laurence, 'A Portrait of the Author as a Bibliography,' 169, 177. See also Laurence's *Bernard Shaw: A Bibliography*, 2 vols. (Oxford: Clarendon Press, 1983); and Purdy, *Thomas Hardy: A Bibliographical Study* (Oxford: Oxford University Press, 1954).
22 Sharon Ouditt, *Women Writers of the First World War*.
23 McKenzie, 'Trading Places? England 1689 – France 1789,' 1.
24 Green, *Print and Protestantism in Early Modern England*, viii.
25 Winship, *American Literary Publishing in the Mid-Nineteenth Century*, 8. Also indispensable for the publishing history of Victorian Britain is Alexis Weedon, *Victorian Publishing*.
26 Blayney, *The Bookshops in Paul's Cross Churchyard*; and *The Stationers' Company before the Charter*. Robin Myers, Michael Harris, and Giles Mandelbrote, eds, *The London Book Trade*, vii–viii.
27 Raven, Garside, and Schöwerling, gen. eds, *The English Novel 1770–1829*, introduction, 1: 120.
28 Fleming and Alston, *Early Canadian Printing*, xviii.
29 Clegg, 'History of the Book,' 245. Similarly Michael Treadwell in 'The History of the Book in Eighteenth-Century England, Ireland, and America' observes: 'The history of the book is an extremely demanding field, not in any lazy, abstract sense of "demanding," but because it constantly and literally demands of us a knowledge of languages that we do not speak or read, of books – some of them bestsellers – of which we have never heard, technologies that we have not mastered, and complex commercial transactions carried on by methods we do not understand in currencies that are never more different than when they seem the same. The laws that govern it all say one thing in the statute books, but mean quite another in practice, and for a quarter of the time, through half the [eighteenth] century, we have to do research to know what year we are in' (134).
30 See below the historian Darnton (31) and the bibliographer Tanselle (32). For 'the new boredom' (as opposed to the new historicism) see David Scott Kastan, *Shakespeare after Theory*, 18. For paleopositivism, etc. (as opposed to the 'sexy knowledge' of cultural studies) see Matthew P. Brown 'Book His-

tory, Sexy Knowledge, and the Challenge of the New Boredom,' 690. For the extreme criticism of literary theory see Jonathan Rose, 'How Historians Teach the History of the Book,' 219–20.
31 Chartier, *The Order of Books*, vii.

Chapter 3 Models of the Book's Place in History

1 Darnton, 'What Is the History of Books?' reprinted in Darnton, *The Kiss of Lamourette*; also reprinted in Cathy Davidson, ed., *Reading in America*; and, slightly abridged, in Finkelstein and McCleery, eds, *The Book History Reader*.
2 Darnton, 'What Is the History of Books?' in *The Kiss of Lamourette*, 108, 111, 135, 113.
3 Ibid., 110.
4 Ibid., 111.
5 For the practice of *l'histoire du livre* in France see Roger Chartier, 'Frenchness in the History of the Book.' Studies date back to 1958, when Lucien Febvre and Henri-Jean Martin's *L'Apparition du livre* was published by Editions Albin Michel. (It was later translated into English as *The Coming of the Book* [1976].) The first of what is now becoming a global library of national histories of the book was Febvre and Chartier, eds., *Histoire de l'édition Française* (1982–6).
6 Darnton, *The Business of Enlightenment*, 2–3.
7 Tanselle, 'From Bibliography to *Histoire totale*,' 647.
8 Howsam, 'Book History Unbound,' 73–4.
9 Raven, *London Booksellers*, xviii.
10 Adams and Barker, 'A New Model,' 6.
11 Ibid., 7.
12 Ibid., 7, 10, 41 n. 26; Kenneth E. Carpenter, ed., *Books and Society in History*, xi.
13 This is not the place for a full discussion of why historians have been reluctant to use objects as evidence, a problem that partly goes back to the establishment in the late nineteenth century of disciplinary boundaries between archaeology and history (but see Philippa Levine, *The Amateur and the Profes-*

sional: Antiquarians, Historians, and Archaeologists in Victorian England, 1838–1886 (Cambridge: Cambridge University Press, 1986). However much the new cultural history has broken down those barriers, along with studies of carnival and other cultural forms in the anthropological sense, there is interest in the objects of desire as identified by cultures in different places across time.

14 Adams and Barker, 'A New Model,' 10.
15 Ibid., 15, 17, 18. They continue: 'The nature of the text and, in some but not all instances, the intention of the authors are factors in this decision, but other forces control it that have little do do with the intrinsic merit of the text.' Intentionality is also addressed in their appendix, 'Intentionality and Reception Theory,' 195–201.
16 Although Ontario public and university libraries were careful to keep and catalogue a wide range of local newspapers, it is remarkably difficult for the historian interested in the social mores of the 1930s to find a complete run of the Toronto scandal sheet *Hush*. See Susan Houston, 'A little steam, a little sizzle and a little sleaze,' 39–40.
17 For consideration of the book as a gendered object see Megan Benton, *Beauty and the Book*; and Howsam, 'In My View: Women and Book History,' 1–2. Matthew P. Brown notes perceptively that 'much McKenzie-inspired scholarship ... celebrates variants for their production of meaning, but ... does not always pursue the sociological dimensions of variants to understand, for instance, sex-gender identities' ('Book History, Sexy Knowledge and the Challenge of the New Boredom,' 694).
18 McDonald, *British Literary Culture and Publishing Practice*, 10, 177 n 37, citing Pierre Bourdieu, *The Field of Cultural Production*, 181–2.
19 McDonald, *British Literary Culture*, 13.
20 Chapter titles of the case studies are: 'Men of letters and children of the sea; Joseph Conrad and the Henley Circle'; 'Playing the field: Arnold Bennett as novelist, serialist and journalist'; and 'Light reading and the dignity of letters:

George Newnes, Ltd. and the making of Arthur Conan Doyle.'
21 McDonald, 'Implicit Structures and Explicit Interactions,' 109.
22 Johns, 'History, Science, and the History of the Book,' 5.
23 Secord, *Victorian Sensation*, 3, 518.
24 Ibid., 515, 532.
25 Steven Shapin and Simon Schaffer, *Leviathan and the Air-Pump: Hobbes, Boyle, and the Experimental Life* (Princeton: Princeton University Press, 1985); Steven Shapin, *A Social History of Truth: Civility and Science in Seventeenth-Century England* (Chicago: University of Chicago Press, 1994).
26 See Joan Shelley Rubin, 'What Is the History of the History of Books?' 555–75, where she suggests that book historians, beginning with Darnton, have limited themselves by drawing artificial distinctions between groups that are actually connected.
27 Darnton, *The Great Cat Massacre*, 155–7.
28 Marina Frasca Spada and Nick Jardine, eds. *Books and the Sciences in History*.

Chapter 4   Where Is *the Book* in History?

1 Darnton, 'An Early Information Society,' 12.
2 The Annales school of history in mid-twentieth century France grew out of a journal, *Annales d'histoire économique et sociale*; its practitioners were interested in developing a quantitative methodology for social history. See Peter Burke, *The French Historical Revolution: The Annales School*.
3 Grafton, 'AHR Forum: How Revolutionary Was the Print Revolution?' 84–5; Chartier, 'Frenchness in the History of the Book,' 308–9.
4 In Asa Briggs and Peter Burke, *A Social History of the Media*, 6, 7.
5 Cited in David Godfrey, 'Introduction' to Harold A. Innis, *Empire and Communications* (Victoria BC: Press Porcépic, 1986).
6 Burke, in Briggs and Burke, *Social History of the Media*, 19. See below for a discussion of the continuation of manuscript cul-

ture deep into the age of the printing press in the work of such scholars as Margaret J.M. Ezell and Harold Love.
7 Burke, in Briggs and Burke, *Social History of the Media*, 21.
8 Johns, *Nature of the Book*, 13.
9 Eisenstein, 'AHR Forum,' 87–105.
10 See, for example, Johns, *Nature of the Book*; Raven, 'New Reading Histories, Print Culture and the Identification of Change,' 286–7; Secord, *Victorian Sensation*.
11 Burke, in Briggs and Burke, *Social History of the Media*, 22.
12 Topham, 'Introduction' to 'Book History and the Sciences,' 153.
13 Johns, 'History, Science, and the History of the Book'; Johns, *Nature of the Book*, 2.
14 Chartier, 'Frenchness in the History of the Book,' 318.
15 This simple but powerful formulation was suggested by William Acres in an address at the University of Windsor in spring 2000 entitled 'History in the Knowledge-Based Economy.'
16 Jordanova, *History in Practice*, 115.
17 S.H. Steinberg, *Five Hundred Years of Printing*, chapter 2.
18 Chartier, 'Frenchness in the History of the Book,' 318–22, sets out three modes of publishing which 'seem to succeed each other' in 'the long-term history of the book.' First, 'publishing as the public performance of a text whose manuscript has been verified and authenticated by the author'; second, the 'typographical ancien regime' from the mid-fifteenth to the first third of the nineteenth century, when 'publishing activity was above all commercial'; and third, 'publishing as an autonomous profession and the publisher as we now know him.' These latter phenomena appeared in France around 1830, and earlier in some places and later in others.
19 Houston, *Literacy in Early Modern Europe*, 231–2; Vincent, *Literacy and Popular Culture*; and Vincent, *The Rise of Mass Literacy*.
20 Chartier, 'Frenchness in the History of the Book,' 308.
21 Raven, 'New Reading Histories,' 281, 286.
22 Kelly-Gadol, 'Did Women Have a Renaissance?' chapter 7.

23 Chartier, 'Frenchness in the History of the Book,' 311.
24 MacDonald and Black, 'Using GIS for Spatial and Temporal Analyses in Print Culture Studies,' 505–36.
25 Anderson, *Imagined Communities*, 34–5, 46. Anderson uses Febvre and Martin, *The Coming of the Book*, as his source for sections on print culture, and in particular their statement that during the fifteenth century twenty million printed books were produced and disseminated. See Joseph Dane's chapter 'Twenty Million Incunables Can't Be Wrong' in *The Myth of Print Culture* for a critique of these figures.
26 McKenzie, 'Trading Places? England 1689 – France 1789,' 22–3.
27 See also Darnton, *Histoire du livre Geschichte des Buchwesens*, 33–41.
28 Chartier, 'Frenchness in the History of the Book,' 304–6.
29 Jacques Michon and Jean-Yves Mollier, eds, *Les Mutations du livre et de l'édition*.
30 'First Contact of Native Peoples with Print Culture,' in Patricia Lockhart Fleming, Gilles Gallichan, and Yvan Lamonde, eds, *History of the Book in Canada*, 1: 13–22. François Melançon, 'La Circulation du livre au Canada sous la domination française.'
31 Germaine Warkentin, 'In Search of "The Word of the Other,"' 4.
32 For circulating libraries see Guinevere L. Griest, *Mudie's Circulating Library*; and Richard D. Altick, *The English Common Reader*.
33 See, among others, Andrew Levy, *The Culture and Commerce of the American Short Story* (Cambridge: Cambridge University Press, 1993); and Michael Lane et al., *Books against Publishers: Commerce against Culture in Postwar Britain* (Lexington, Ky: Lexington Books, 1980). See also N.N. Feltes' work on the 'commodity text' in *Modes of Production of Victorian Novels* and *Literary Capital and the Late Victorian Novel*.
34 Raven, 'British Publishing and Bookselling.' See also Raven, 'The Structure of Publishing and Bookselling in Victorian Britain.' Forthcoming in 2006 is Raven's *The Commercialization*

of the Book: Booksellers and the Commodification of Literature in Britain 1450 to 1900.

35 Raven, ed., *Free Print and Non-commercial Publishing since 1700.*
36 Bruno Latour and his followers refer to the laboratory as a 'system of literary inscription.' For acts of 'inscription' see also Timothy Lenoir, ed., *Inscribing Science: Scientific Texts and the Materiality of Communication* (Stanford: Stanford University Press, 1998); and Mario Biagioli and Peter Galison, eds, *Scientific Authorship*. I am grateful to Jennifer Connor for these references.
37 On copyright see James J. Barnes, *Authors, Publishers, and Politicians*. On literary property more broadly see Eva Hemmungs Wirtén, *No Trespassing*; and William St Clair, *The Reading Nation*.
38 Edward H. Jacobs comments that 'book historians have made almost no attempt to specify what past people actually did when they selected books from catalogues and bookshops' ('Buying into Classes,' 43–64). See also Louis-George Harvey, 'Writing the History of Readers.' In a comment on Darnton's communication circuit Harvey notes: 'In terms of the social history of ideas, however, one could argue that the distribution and consumption stage of the book's "life cycle" are potentially the most revealing. For these activities encompass the interaction of the reader and the book, and allow us to evaluate the book's impact, and, conversely, the impact of the aggregate demand created by readers on the other stages of the communication *circuit*. Having said this, the analysis of distribution and consumption is no easy task, for it involves studying the activities of publishers, booksellers and their agents, as well as those of readers. What is more, such an emphasis leads us to consider other important variables, such as price and supply of printed materials, censorship and, of course, literacy.'
39 On the consumption of books see Radway, 'Reading Is Not Eating,' 7–29.
40 Darnton, *The Business of Enlightenment*, 2. Kathryn Hughes, *The Short Life and Long Times of Mrs Beeton* (London: Fourth Estate,

2005). Leslie Howsam, 'Food for Thought [Mrs Beeton's Books],' *Rare Book Review* 31, no. 3 (April 2004): 32–6.
41 Brown, 'Book History, Sexy Knowledge, and the Challenge of the New Boredom,' 703.

Chapter 5   Cross-Disciplinary Observations

1 Robbie McClintock, 'Social History through Media History,' [review of Briggs and Burke, *A Social History of the Media*, and Burke, *A Social History of Knowledge*], *The Study Place: Explorations in Education* (2002); www.studyplace.org/readings/.
2 Anthony Grafton, 'The Importance of Being Printed.' For a checklist of reviews see Peter McNally, *The Advent of Printing*. See also Joseph A. Dane, *The Myth of Print Culture*, 11–21, for a discussion of Eisenstein and Johns.
3 See for example Thomas F.X. Noble et al., *Western Civilization: The Continuing Experiment*, 2nd ed (Boston: Houghton Mifflin, 1998), 472.
4 Raven, 'New Reading Histories,' 183.
5 Eisenstein, *The Printing Press As an Agent of Change*, xii.
6 Eisenstein, 'AHR Forum,' 88.
7 Johns, 'AHR Forum,' 116.
8 Grafton, 'AHR Forum,' 86.
9 Johns, 'AHR Forum,' 110.
10 See also Guglielmo Cavallo and Roger Chartier, eds, *A History of Reading in the West*. In 'Frenchness in the History of the Book' Chartier notes the fundamental distinctions between reading aloud and reading silently; between reading in solitude and public reading; and between 'educated reading and "popular" reading' (322–4).
11 Sharpe, *Reading Revolutions*, 40.
12 McKitterick, *Print, Manuscript and the Search for Order*, 3, 217–18, 8, 222.
13 Eisenstein, 'AHR Forum,' 93.
14 McKitterick, *Print, Manuscript and the Search for Order*, 102.
15 Ibid., 117–18, 132–3, 223, 227.
16 The origins of bibliography have been placed much earlier,

some say in Alexandria while others insist on the evidence of editorial and critical bibliography in the Renaissance; one great textual critic was Angelo Poliziano. I am grateful to Germaine Warkentin for pointing this out to me.
17 Eggert, 'Textual Product or Textual Process,' 29.
18 Marcus, *Unediting the Renaissance*, 1.
19 Ibid., 2, 25.
20 Ibid., 27.
21 Perkins, *Is Literary History Possible?* 12, 17.
22 Ibid., 177.
23 Clifford Geertz, 'Thick Description: Towards an Interpretive Theory of Culture,' in Geertz, ed., *The Interpretation of Cultures* (1975), quoted in David Vincent, *Literacy and Popular Culture*, 4.
24 Johns, *The Nature of the Book*, 623.
25 Sharpe, *Reading Revolutions*, 39–40. Sharpe mentions Darnton's *The Business of Enlightenment* (1979) as an example of work by a 'mainstream' historian. The passage continues: 'This is perhaps a particular danger in England where intellectual history of a traditional stripe has shown itself disinclined to study what we might call the material culture of ideas: books, bindings, library furniture, leaving such subjects to more artisanal colleagues, less at home in the rarefied world of Platonic philosophy or natural rights theory. It may be no accident that the continental, German and French, inclination to theory and an American comfort with (what the English still regard as vulgar) consumerism, along with a more democratic even populist ideology, have combined to produce the best scholarship in the history of reading.'
26 Rabinowitz, *Before Reading*, 2.

Bibliography

Adams, Thomas R., and Nicolas Barker. 'A New Model for the Study of the Book.' In *A Potencie of Life: Books in Society*, edited by Nicolas Barker, 5–43. London: British Library, 1993.

Allan, David. 'Some Methods and Problems in the History of Reading: Georgian England and the Scottish Enlightenment.' *Journal of the Historical Society* 3, no. 1 (Winter 2003): 9–124.

Altick, Richard D. *The English Common Reader: A Social History of the Mass Reading Public, 1800–1900*. Chicago: University of Chicago Press, 1957.

Amory, Hugh. 'Physical Bibliography, Cultural History, and the Disappearance of the Book.' *Papers of the Bibliographical Society of America* 78, no. 3 (1984): 341–7.

Anderson, Benedict. *Imagined Communities: Reflections on the Origin and Spread of Nationalism*. Revised edition. London: Verso, 1991.

Barker, Nicolas. *Form and Meaning in the History of the Book*. London: British Library, 2003.

Barnes, James J. *Authors, Publishers, and Politicians: The Quest for an Anglo-American Copyright Agreement, 1815–1854*. Columbus: Ohio State University Press, 1974.

Bell, Bill. 'New Directions in Victorian Publishing History.' *Victorian Literature and Culture* 22 (1994): 347–54.

Bell, Bill, Philip Bennett, and Jonquil Bevan, eds. *Across Boundaries: The Book in Culture and Commerce*. Winchester, Hampshire: St Paul's Bibliographies / New Castle, Del.: Oak Knoll Press, 2000.

Bibliography

Benton, Megan. *Beauty and the Book: Fine Editions and Cultural Distinction in America.* New Haven: Yale University Press, 2000.

Biagioli, Mario, and Peter Galison, eds. *Scientific Authorship: Cultural and Intellectual Property in Science.* New York: Routledge, 2003.

Blayney, Peter W.M. *The Bookshops in Paul's Cross Churchyard.* London: Bibliographical Society, 1990.

– *The Stationers' Company before the Charter, 1403–1557.* London: Worshipful Company of Stationers and Newspapermakers, 2003.

Bourdieu, Pierre. *The Field of Cultural Production.* Edited by Randal Johnson. Cambridge: Polity Press, 1993.

Brake, Laurel. *Print in Transition, 1850–1910: Studies in Media and Book History.* London: Palgrave, 2001.

Briggs, Asa, and Peter Burke. *A Social History of the Media: From Gutenberg to the Internet.* Cambridge: Polity Press, 2002.

Brown, Matthew P. 'Book History, Sexy Knowledge, and the Challenge of the New Boredom.' *American Literary History* 16, no. 4 (2004): 688–706.

Burke, Peter. *The French Historical Revolution: The Annales School, 1929–89.* London: Polity Press, 1990.

– *A Social History of Knowledge: From Gutenberg to Diderot.* Cambridge: Polity Press, 2000.

Carpenter, Kenneth E., ed. *Books and Society in History.* Papers of the Association of College and Research Libraries Rare Books and Manuscripts Conference, 24–8 June 1980. New York: Bowker, 1983.

Casper, Scott E. *Constructing American Lives: Biography and Culture in Nineteenth-Century America.* Chapel Hill: University of North Carolina Press, 1999.

Casper, Scott E., Joanne D. Chaison, and Jeffrey D. Groves, eds. *Perspectives on American Book History: Artifacts and Commentary.* Amherst: University of Massachusetts Press, 2002.

Cavallo, Guglielmo, and Roger Chartier, eds. *A History of Reading in the West.* Studies in Print Culture and the History of the Book. Amherst: University of Massachussets Press, 1999.

Chartier, Roger. 'Frenchness in the History of the Book: From

the History of Publishing to the History of Reading.' *Proceedings of the American Antiquarian Society* 97, no. 2 (1987): 299–329.
- *The Order of Books: Readers, Authors, and Libraries in Europe between the Fourteenth and Eighteenth Centuries.* Translated by Lydia G. Cochrane. Originally published in 1992 as *L'Ordre des livres.* Cambridge: Polity Press / Stanford, Calif.: Stanford University Press, 1994.

Clegg, Cyndia. 'History of the Book: An Undisciplined Discipline?' Review essay in *Renaissance Quarterly* 54 (2001): 221–45.

Dane, Joseph A. *The Myth of Print Culture: Essays on Evidence, Textuality, and Bibliographical Method.* Toronto: University of Toronto Press, 2003.

Danky, James P., and Wayne A. Wiegand, eds. *Print Culture in a Diverse America.* Urbana: University of Illinois Press, 1998.

Darnton, Robert. *The Business of Enlightenment: A Publishing History of the Encyclopédie 1775–1800.* Cambridge, Mass.: Belknap Press of Harvard University Press, 1979.
- 'What Is the History of Books?' *Daedalus* 111, no. 3 (1982): 65–83. Reprinted as chapter 7 in *The Kiss of Lamourette: Reflections in Cultural History.* New York: Norton, 1990. Citations in this volume are to *The Kiss of Lamourette..*
- *The Great Cat Massacre and Other Episodes of French Cultural History.* New York: Basic Books, 1984.
- '*Histoire du livre Geschichte des Buchwesens*: An Agenda for Comparative History.' *Publishing History* 22 (1987): 33–41.
- *The Forbidden Best-Sellers of Pre-Revolutionary France.* New York: Norton, 1995.
- 'An Early Information Society: News and the Media in Eighteenth-Century Paris.' *American Historical Review* 105, no. 1 (February 2000): 1–35; http://www.indiana.edu/~ahr/darnton/.
- 'History of reading.' In Peter Burke, ed., *New Perspectives on Historical Writing*, 157–86. 2nd edition. University Park: Pennsylvania State University Press, 2001. Originally published in the *Australian Journal of French Studies* 23 (1986): 5–30.

Davidson, Cathy. *Revolution and the Word: The Rise of the Novel in America.* New York: Oxford University Press, 1986.

– ed. *Reading in America: Literature and Social History.* Baltimore: Johns Hopkins University Press, 1989.

Dooley, Allan C. *Author and Printer in Victorian England.* Char-. lottesville: University Press of Virginia, 1992.

Eggert, Paul. 'Textual Product or Textual Process: Procedures and Assumptions of Critical Editing.' In Paul Eggert, ed., *Editing in Australia*, 19–44. Canberra : New South Wales University Press, 1990.

Eisenstein, Elizabeth L. *The Printing Press As an Agent of Change: Communications and Cultural Transformations in Early Modern Europe.* New York: Cambridge University Press, 1979. Abridged without documentation as *The Printing Revolution in Early Modern Europe* (Cambridge: Cambridge University Press, 1984).

– 'AHR Forum: An Unacknowledged Revolution Revisited.' *American Historical Review* 107 (February 2002): 87–105.

Eliot, Simon. *Some Patterns and Trends in British Publishing 1800–1919.* Occasional Papers of the Bibliographical Society 8. London: The Bibliographical Society, 1994.

– '*Patterns and Trends and the NSTC*: Some Initial Observations. Part One.' *Publishing History* 42 (1997): 79–104.

– '*Patterns and Trends and the NSTC*: Some Initial Observations. Part Two.' *Publishing History* 43 (1998): 71–112.

Ezell, Margaret J.M. *Writing Women's Literary History.* Baltimore: Johns Hopkins University Press, 1993.

– *Social Authorship and the Advent of Print.* Baltimore: Johns Hopkins University Press, 1999.

Feather, John. 'Cross-Channel Currents: Historical Bibliography and *L'Histoire du livre.*' *The Library* 6th series, 2, no. 1 (1980): 1–15.

– *A History of British Publishing.* London: Routledge, 1988.

Febvre, Lucien, and Henri-Jean Martin. *The Coming of the Book: The Impact of Printing 1450–1800.* London: NLB / New York: Schocken, 1976.

Febvre, Lucien, and Roger Chartier, eds. *Histoire de l'édition française.* 4 volumes. Paris: Promodis, 1982–6.

Feltes, N.N. *Modes of Production of Victorian Novels.* Chicago: University of Chicago Press, 1986.

- *Literary Capital and the Late Victorian Novel.* Madison: University of Wisconsin Press, 1993.
Finkelstein, David. *The House of Blackwood: Author-Publisher Relations in the Victorian Era.* University Park: Pennsylvania State University Press, 2002.
Finkelstein, David, and Alistair McCleery. *An Introduction to Book History.* London: Routledge, 2005.
- eds. *The Book History Reader.* London: Routledge, 2002.
Fish, Stanley. *Is There a Text in This Class?* Cambridge: Harvard University Press, 1980.
Fleming, Patricia L., and Sandra Alston. *Early Canadian Printing: A Supplement to Marie Tremaine's A Bibliography of Canadian Imprints, 1751–1800.* Toronto: University of Toronto Press, 1999.
Fleming, Patricia L., Gilles Gallichan, and Yvan Lamonde, eds. *History of the Book in Canada.* Volume 1: *Beginnings to 1840.* Toronto: University of Toronto Press, 2004.
Flint, Kate. *The Woman Reader.* New York: Oxford University Press, 1993.
Frasca Spada, Marina, and Nick Jardine. *Books and the Sciences in History.* Cambridge: Cambridge University Press, 2000.
Fuller, Danielle, and DeNel R. Sedo. 'A Reading Spectacle for the Nation: The CBC and "Canada Reads."' *Journal of Canadian Studies* 40, no. 1 (2006): 5–36.
Fyfe, Aileen. *Industrialised Conversion: The Religious Tract Society and Popular Science Publishing in Victorian Britain.* Cambridge: Cambridge University Press, 2000.
Gardiner, Juliet. 'Recuperating the Author: Consuming Fictions of the 1990s.' *Proceedings of the Bibliographical Society of America* 94, no. 2 (2000): 255–74.
Gaskell, Philip. *A New Introduction to Bibliography.* Oxford: Oxford University Press, 1972.
Grafton, Anthony. 'The Importance of Being Printed.' *Journal of Interdisciplinary History* 11, no. 2 (Autumn 1980): 265–86.
- 'Is the History of Reading a Marginal Enterprise? Guillaume Budé and His Books.' *Papers of the Bibliographical Society of America* 91, no. 2 (1997): 139–57.

- 'AHR Forum: How Revolutionary Was the Print Revolution?' *American Historical Review* 107 (February 2002): 84–6.
- Green, Ian. *Print and Protestantism in Early Modern England.* Oxford: Oxford University Press, 2000.
- Greetham, D.C. *Theories of the Text.* Oxford: Oxford University Press, 1999.
- Griest, Guinevere L. *Mudie's Circulating Library and the Victorian Novel.* Bloomington: Indiana University Press, 1970.
- Hall, David D. 'On Native Ground: From the History of Printing to the History of the Book.' *Proceedings of the American Antiquarian Society* 93 (1983): 313–36.
- *Cultures of Print: Essays in the History of the Book.* Amherst: University of Massachusetts Press, 1996.
- Harvey, Louis-George. 'Writing the History of Readers: *Historie du livre* and the Social History of Ideas in America.' *Journal of History and Politics* 6 (1988–9): 155–77.
- Hemmungs Wirtén, Eva. *No Trespassing: Authorship, Intellectual Property Rights, and the Boundaries of Globalization.* Toronto: University of Toronto Press, 2004.
- Houston, R.A. *Literacy in Early Modern Europe: Culture and Education 1500–1800.* London: Longman, 1988.
- Houston, Susan. '"A little steam, a little sizzle and a little sleaze": English-Language Tabloids in the Interwar Period.' *Papers of the Bibliographical Society of Canada* 40, no. 1 (2002): 37–60.
- Howsam, Leslie. *Cheap Bibles: Nineteenth-Century Publishing and the British and Foreign Bible Society.* Cambridge: Cambridge University Press, 1991.
- 'Victorian Studies and the History of the Book: Opportunities for Scholarly Collaboration.' *Victorian Review* 22, no. 1 (1996): 65–70.
- 'In My View: Women and Book History' (Guest Editorial). *SHARP News* 7, no. 4 (Autumn 1998): 1–2.
- 'An Experiment with Science for the Nineteenth-Century Book Trade: The International Scientific Series.' *British Journal for the History of Science* 33 (2000): 187–207.

- 'Book History Unbound: Transactions of the Written Word Made Public.' *Canadian Journal of History / Annales canadiennes d'histoire* 38 (April/avril 2003): 69–81.
Hudson, Nicholas. 'Challenging Eisenstein: Recent Studies in Print Culture.' *Eighteenth-Century Life* 26, no. 2 (Spring 2002): 83–95.
Iser, Wolfgang. *The Act of Reading: A Theory of Aesthetic Response.* Baltimore: Johns Hopkins University Press, 1978.
- *The Implied Reader: Patterns of Communication in Prose Fiction from Bunyan to Beckett.* Baltimore: Johns Hopkins University Press, 1978.
Jackson, H.J. *Marginalia: Readers Writing in Books.* New Haven: Yale University Press, 2001.
- *Romantic Readers: The Evidence of Marginalia.* New Haven: Yale University Press, 2005.
Jacobs, Edward H. 'Buying into Classes: The Practice of Book Selection in Eighteenth-Century Britain.' *Eighteenth-Century Studies* 33, no. 1 (1999): 43–64.
Jauss, Hans Robert. *Towards an Aesthetic of Reception.* Minneapolis: University of Minnesota Press, 1982.
Johns, Adrian. 'History, Science, and the History of the Book: The Making of Natural Philosophy in Early Modern England.' *Publishing History* 30 (1994): 3–30.
- *The Nature of the Book: Print and Knowledge in the Making.* Chicago: University of Chicago Press, 1998.
- 'AHR Forum: How to Acknowledge a Revolution.' *American Historical Review* 107 (February 2002): 106–25.
Johnson, William A. *Bookrolls and Scribes in Oxyrhynchus.* Toronto: University of Toronto Press, 2004.
Jordan, John O., and Robert L. Patten, eds. *Literature in the Marketplace: Nineteenth-Century British Publishing and Reading Practices.* Cambridge: Cambridge University Press, 1995.
Jordanova, Ludmilla. *History in Practice.* London: Arnold, 2000.
Kastan, David Scott. *Shakespeare after Theory.* New York: Routledge, 1999.
Kelly-Gadol, Joan. 'Did Women Have a Renaissance?' In *Becoming*

Visible: Women in European History, edited by Renate Bridenthal and Claudia Koonz, chapter 7. 2nd edition. Boston: Houghton Mifflin, 1987.

Laurence, Dan H. 'A Portrait of the Author as a Bibliography.' *Book Collector* 35 (Summer 1986): 165–77.

Love, Harold. *Scribal Publication in Seventeenth-Century England*. Oxford: Clarendon Press, 1993.

MacDonald, Bertrum H., and Fiona A. Black. 'Using GIS for Spatial and Temporal Analyses in Print Culture Studies: Some Opportunities and Challenges.' *Social Science History* 24, no. 3 (Fall 2000): 505–36.

Manguel, Alberto. *A History of Reading*. Toronto: Knopf, 1996.

Marcus, Leah S. *Unediting the Renaissance: Shakespeare, Marlowe, Milton*. London: Routledge, 1996.

Martin, Henri-Jean. *The History and Power of Writing*. Translated by Lydia G. Cochrane. Chicago: University of Chicago Press, 1994.

Martin, Henri-Jean, et al., eds. *Histoire de l'édition française*. 4 volumes. Paris: Promodis, 1982–6.

McDonald, Peter D. *British Literary Culture and Publishing Practice, 1880–1914*. Cambridge: Cambridge University Press, 1997.

– 'Implicit Structures and Explicit Interactions: Pierre Bourdieu and the History of the Book.' *The Library* 6th series, 19, no. 2 (1997): 105–21.

McGann, Jerome. *The Textual Condition*. Princeton: Princeton University Press, 1991.

– 'Visible and Invisible Books: Hermetic Images in N-Dimensional Space.' In *The Future of the Page*, edited by Peter Stoicheff and Andrew Taylor. Toronto: University of Toronto Press, 2004.

McGill, Meredith L. *American Literature and the Culture of Reprinting, 1834–1853*. Philadelphia: University of Pennsylvania Press, 2003.

McKenzie, D.F. 'The Sociology of a Text: Orality, Literacy and Print in Early New Zealand.' *The Library* 6th series, 6 (1984): 333–65. Reprinted in D.F. McKenzie, *Bibliography and the Sociology of Texts* (Cambridge: Cambridge University Press, 1999).

– *Bibliography and the Sociology of Texts*. Panizzi Lectures 1985.

London: British Library 1986. Reprinted in D.F. McKenzie, *Bibliography and the Sociology of Texts* (Cambridge: Cambridge University Press, 1999).
- 'Trading Places? England 1689 – France 1789.' In *The Darnton Debate: Books and Revolution in the Eighteenth Century*, edited by Haydn T. Mason. Oxford: Voltaire Foundation, 1998. Reprinted in D.F. McKenzie, *Making Meaning: "Printers of the Mind" and Other Essays*, edited by Peter D. McDonald and Michael F. Suarez, 144–65 (Amherst: University of Massachusetts Press, 2002).

McKerrow, Ronald B. *An Introduction to Bibliography for Literary Students*. Oxford: Clarendon Press, 1927.

McKitterick, David. *Print, Manuscript and the Search for Order, 1450–1830*. Cambridge: Cambridge University Press, 2003.

McNally, Peter. *The Advent of Printing: Historians of Science Respond to Elizabeth Eisenstein's 'The Printing Press as an Agent of Change.'* Montreal: McGill University Graduate School of Library and Information Studies, 1987.

Melançon, François. 'La Circulation du livre au Canada sous la domination française.' *Papers of the Bibliographical Society of Canada / Cahiers de la Société bibliographique du Canada* 37, no. 2 (1999): 35–58.

Michon, Jacques, and Jean-Yves Mollier, eds. *Les Mutations du livre et de l'édition dans le monde du XVIIIe siècle à l'An 2000*. Québec: Presses de l'Université Laval, 2001.

Moylan, Michele, and Lane Stiles, eds. *Reading Books: Essays on the Material Text and Literature in America*. Amherst: University of Massachusetts Press, 1996.

Murray, Heather. *Come, bright Improvement! The Literary Societies of Nineteenth-Century Ontario*. Toronto: University of Toronto Press, 2002.

Myers, Robin, Michael Harris, and Giles Mandelbrote. *The London Book Trade: Topographies of Print in the Metropolis from the Sixteenth Century*. New Castle, Del.: Oak Knoll Press / London: British Library, 2003.

Ouditt, Sharon. *Women Writers of the First World War: An Annotated Bibliography*. London: Routledge, 2000.

Patten, Robert L. *Charles Dickens and His Publishers.* Oxford: Clarendon Press, 1978.

Perkins, David. *Is Literary History Possible?* Baltimore: Johns Hopkins University Press, 1992.

Rabinowitz, Peter J. *Before Reading: Narrative Conventions and the Politics of Interpretation.* Ithaca: Cornell University Press, 1987.

Radway, Janice A. *Reading the Romance: Women, Patriarchy and Popular Culture.* Chapel Hill: University of North Carolina Press, 1984. Reprinted with a new introduction 1991.

– 'Reading Is Not Eating: Mass-Produced Literature and the Theoretical, Methodological, and Political Consequences of a Metaphor.' *Book Research Quarterly* 2 (Fall 1986): 7–29.

– *A Feeling for Books: The Book-of-the-Month Club, Literary Taste, and Middle-Class Desire.* Chapel Hill: University of North Carolina Press, 1997.

Raven, James. 'New Reading Histories, Print Culture and the Identification of Change: The Case of Eighteenth-Century England.' *Social History* 23, no. 3 (1998): 268–87.

– 'British Publishing and Bookselling: Constraints and Developments.' In Michon and Mollier, eds, *Les Mutations du livre* (2001), 19–30.

– *London Booksellers and American Customers: Transatlantic Literary Community and the Charleston Library Society, 1748–1811.* Columbia: University of South Carolina Press, 2002.

– 'The Structure of Publishing and Bookselling in Victorian Britain.' In Martin Daunton, ed., *The Organization of Knowledge in Victorian Britain*, chapter 12. London: British Academy, 2004.

– ed. *Free Print and Non-Commercial Publishing since 1700.* London: Ashgate Publishing, 2000.

Raven, James, Peter Garside, and Rainer Schöwerling, gen. eds. *The English Novel 1770–1829: A Bibliographical Survey of Prose Fiction Published in the British Isles.* Volume 1: *1770–1799*, edited by James Raven and Antonia Forster; volume 2: *1800–1829*, edited by Peter Garside and Rainer Schöwerling. Oxford: Oxford University Press, 2000.

Raven, James, Helen Small, and Naomi Tadmor, eds. *The Practice*

and Representation of Reading in England. Cambridge: Cambridge University Press, 1996.
Rivers, Isabel. *Books and Readers in Eighteenth-Century England: New Essays.* London: Leicester University Press, 2001.
Rose, Jonathan. 'Rereading the English Common Reader: A Preface to a History of Audiences.' *Journal of the History of Ideas* 53 (1992): 47–70.
– 'How Historians Teach the History of the Book.' *Canadian Review of Comparative Literature / Revue canadienne de littérature comparée* 23, no. 1 (March 1996): 219–20.
– *The Intellectual History of the British Working Classes.* New Haven: Yale University Press, 2001.
– 'The Horizon of a New Discipline: Inventing Book Studies.' *Publishing Research Quarterly* 19 (Spring 2003): 11–19.
Rubin, Joan Shelley. 'What Is the History of the History of Books?' *Journal of American History* 90, no. 2 (2003): 555–75.
Ryan, Barbara. *Reading Acts: U.S. Readers' Interactions with Literature, 1800–1950.* Knoxville: University of Tennessee Press, 2002.
St Clair, William. *The Reading Nation in the Romantic Period.* Cambridge: Cambridge University Press, 2004.
Sauer, Elizabeth. *'Paper-Contestations' and Textual Communities in England, 1640–1675.* Toronto: University of Toronto Press, 2005.
Secord, James A. *Victorian Sensation: The Extraordinary Publication, Reception, and Secret Authorship of 'Vestiges of the Natural History of Creation.'* Chicago: University of Chicago Press, 2000.
Sharpe, Kevin. *Reading Revolutions: The Politics of Reading in Early Modern England.* New Haven: Yale University Press, 2000.
Shillingsburg, P.L. *Pegasus in Harness: Victorian Publishing and W.M. Thackeray.* Charlottesville: University Press of Virginia, 1992.
Steinberg, S.H. *Five Hundred Years of Printing.* Revised by John Trevitt. London: British Library / New Castle, Del.: Oak Knoll Press, 1996. First published 1955.
Stoddard, Roger E. 'Morphology and the Book from an American Perspective.' *Printing History* 9, no. 1 (1987): 2–14.
Stoicheff, Peter, and Andrew Taylor, eds. *The Future of the Page.* Toronto: University of Toronto Press, 2004.

Suleiman, Susan K., and Inge Crossman, eds. *The Reader in the Text: Essays on Audience and Interpretation*. Princeton: Princeton University Press, 1980.

Sutherland, J.A. *Victorian Novelists and Publishers*. London: Athlone / Chicago: University of Chicago Press, 1976.

– 'Publishing History: A Hole at the Center of Literary Sociology.' *Critical Inquiry* 14 (Spring 1988): 574–89.

Tanselle, G. Thomas. 'From Bibliography to *Histoire totale*: The History of Books As a Field of Study.' *Times Literary Supplement*, 5 June 1981.

– *Literature and Artifacts*. Charlottesville: Bibliographical Society of the University of Virginia, 1998.

Thompson, Edward P. *The Making of the English Working Class*. Harmondsworth: Penguin, 1998.

Topham, Jonathan. 'Beyond the "Common Context": The Production and Reading of the *Bridgewater Treatises*.' *Isis* 89 (1998): 233–62.

– 'Introduction' to 'Book History and the Sciences,' a special section of *British Journal for the History of Science* 33 (June 2000): 155–8.

– 'Scientific Publishing and the Reading of Science in Nineteenth-Century Britain: A Historiographical Survey and Guide to Sources.' *Studies in the History and Philosophy of Science* 31, no. 4 (2000): 559–612.

Treadwell, Michael. 'Review Essay: The History of the Book . in Eighteenth-Century England, Ireland, and America.' *Eighteenth-Century Life* 16 (May 1992): 110–35.

Vincent, David. *Bread, Knowledge and Freedom: A Study of . Nineteenth-Century Working Class Autobiography*. London: Methuen, 1981.

– *Literacy and Popular Culture: England 1750–1914*. Cambridge: Cambridge University Press, 1989.

– *The Rise of Mass Literacy: Reading and Writing in Modern Europe*. Cambridge: Polity Press, 2000.

Warkentin, Germaine. 'In Search of "The Word of the Other": Aboriginal Sign Systems and the History of the Book in Canada.' *Book History* 2 (1999): 1–27.

Webb, R.K. *The British Working-Class Reader 1790–1848: Literacy and Social Tension.* New York: A.M. Kelley, 1971.

Weedon, Alexis. *Victorian Publishing: The Economics of Book Production for a Mass Market, 1836–1916.* Aldershot: Ashgate, 2003.

Winship, Michael. *American Literary Publishing in the Mid-Nineteenth Century: The Business of Ticknor and Fields.* Cambridge: Cambridge University Press, 1995.

Zboray, Ronald J., and Mary Saracino Zboray. *Literary Dollars and Social Sense: A People's History of the Mass Market Book.* New York: Routledge, 2005.

Index

Adams, Thomas R., and Nicolas Barker, 14–15, 33–5, 37, 39, 48, 86n15
agency, 12, 15, 33, 46–8, 51–2, 61–5
Allan, David, 19, 22, 80n15
Alston, Sandra. *See* Fleming, Patricia L., and Sandra Alston
Altick, Richard D., 89n32
Anderson, Benedict, 58, 77, 89n25
Annales. See *histoire du livre*
archives, publishers', 14, 33, 77
art, history of, 29, 76
authorship, history of, 4, 6, 8, 17, 21, 39, 62–3

Barker, Nicolas, 36, 82n5. *See also* Adams, Thomas R., and Nicolas Barker
Barnes, James J., 90n37
Barthes, Roland, 7, 71, 80n10
Benton, Megan, 86n17

bibles. *See* religion
bibliography, 4, 13–15, 17, 20, 24–7, 33–8, 68–70; as a branch of history, 32, 34–5; as the sociology of texts, 17, 20–1, 83n14; analytical, 14, 32; degressive 15, 34; historical, 15; imprint, 17, 25–6; single-author 17, 23–4
biography, 12–13, 16, 41
Black, Fiona, 57
Blayney, Peter, 25, 57
book culture, 12–13, 16, 41
book trade history, 17, 25, 57–8
Bourdieu, Pierre, 38–40, 86n18
Bowers, Fredson, 70
broadcast media, 6, 51, 71
Brown, Matthew P., 64, 84n30, 86n17
Burke, Peter, 49, 50–1, 87n2, 91n1

Carpenter, Kenneth E., 85n12

Index

Casper, Scott E.,16
Cavallo, Guglielmo, 91n10
censorship, 61–2
Chartier, Roger, 27, 52–6, 59, 85n5, 88n18, 91n10
class. *See* identity
Clegg, Cyndia, 6, 9, 26, 76–7
collecting, 8, 23, 37
commerce, 5–6, 48, 58, 62
communication, 6, 49–50, 53–64 passim, 74
communication circuit. *See* Darnton, Robert
cultural studies, 6, 17, 19–20

Dane, Joseph A., 82n5, 89n25, 91n2
Danky, James P., and Wayne Wiegand, 82n6
Darnton, Robert, 6, 8, 25, 43, 45, 59, 62, 64, 76–7, 84n30, 90n38, 92n25; communication circuit, 28–35, 37–41, 47, 72–3
Davidson, Cathy, 21
definitions. *See* terminology
digital culture, 5–7, 71
discipline, 4, 72–7 passim

Eggert, Paul, 70
Eisenstein, Elizabeth, 33, 48, 50, 65. *See also* Eisenstein-Johns debate
Eisenstein-Johns debate, 65–9, 79n9, 91n2
electronic texts, 3, 6, 63, 72
Ezell, Margaret J.M., 18, 88n6

Febvre, Lucien, 47, 57, 85n5, 89n25
Feltes, N.N., 89n33
Finkelstein, David, 25. *See also* Finkelstein, David, and Alistair McCleery
Finkelstein, David, and Alistair McCleery, 79n1
fixity of text. *See* mutability
Fleming, Patricia L., and Sandra Alston, 26
Foucault, Michel, 7, 80n10
Fuller, Danielle, and DeNel R. Sedo, 82n9

Gardiner, Juliet, 80n10, 82n9
Gaskell, Philip, 81n21
gender. *See* identity
Geographic Information Systems, 57
Grafton, Anthony, 47, 83n19
Green, Ian, 24
Greetham, D.C., 11, 81n16
Greg, W.W., 70
Griest, Guinevere L., 89n32

Harris, Michael. *See* Myers, Robin, and Michael Harris
Harvey, Louis-George, 90n38
Hemmungs Wirtén, Eva, 90n37
histoire du livre, 5, 31–2, 47, 55, 59, 74, 87n2
history, 4, 6, 9–12, 24–7, 32–3, 46–64 passim; cultural, 12–13, 16–17, 33, 45, 48, 59, 74, 86n13. *See also* agency; art,

Index 109

history of; literary history; science, history of
Houston, R.A., 55
Houston, Susan., 86n16
Howsam, Leslie, 25

identity, 5, 12, 18, 32, 37–8, 47–8, 50, 55, 59, 77
Innis, Harold, 49–50
intellectual property, 22, 43
interdisciplinarity, 4–9, 26–7, 29, 31, 35, 37, 72–7 passim
Iser, Wolfgang, 82n10

Jackson, H.J., 22, 83n19
Jacobs, Edward H., 90n38
Jauss, Hans Robert, 82n10
Johns, Adrian, 41, 52–3, 67, 71, 74–5, 88n10. *See also* Eisenstein-Johns debate
Jordanova, Ludmilla, 11, 53

Kastan, David Scott, 84n30
Kelly-Gadol, Joan, 56–7

Laurence, Dan H., 23–4
libraries, 6, 13, 37, 62, 89n32
literacy, 20, 46, 54–6, 90n38
literary criticism, 11, 18, 40, 73–4. *See also* theory
literary history, 17–18, 73–4
literary replication. *See* Secord, James
literature, 4, 6, 9–12, 20–4, 38–40. *See also* literary criticism; literary history; text
Love, Harold, 88n6

MacDonald, Bertrum H., 57
manuscript culture, 29, 49–50, 54, 56, 60–1, 68–70
mapping of book cultures, 35, 57
Marcus, Leah S., 70–1
marginalia, 13, 14, 21–2, 83n19
Martin, Henri-Jean, 56–7, 85n5, 89n25
material object, book as a, 4, 6–7, 11, 15, 19, 21–2, 46, 56–7. *See also* bibliography
McCleery, Alastair. *See* Finkelstein, David, and Alistair McCleery
McClintock, Robbie, 64
McDonald, Peter D., 38–42
McGann, Jerome, 9, 21, 70
McGill, Meredith L., 18
McKenzie, D.F., 7, 15, 24, 33–4, 59, 70, 77, 86n17. *See also* bibliography: as the sociology of texts
McKerrow, Ronald B., 82n13
McKitterick, David, 68–9, 71
McLuhan, Marshall, 48–51, 65
McNally, Peter, 91n2
media. *See* broadcast media
Melançon, François, 61
Michon, Jacques, and Jean-Yves Mollier, 89n29
Mollier, Jean-Yves. *See* Michon, Jacques, and Jean-Yves Mollier
Moylan, Michele, and Lane Stiles, 9, 21, 80n13, 83n16

mutability of the book form, 7, 51, 65–77 passim
Myers, Robin, and Michael Harris, 25

national histories of the book, 57–61
national identity. *See* identity
new historicism, 11, 81n15
newspapers. *See* periodicals
non-fiction, 63–4

Ong, Walter, 50
oral culture, 5, 49–50, 54
Ouditt, Sharon, 84n22

Patten, Robert L., 21
periodicals, 5, 18, 58, 86n16
periodization, 53–5
Perkins, David, 18, 73–4
pictographic. *See* sign systems
piracy. *See* intellectual property
politics, history of, 12, 23, 25, 32, 58, 67–8
Pollard, Alfred, 70
print culture, 17–19, 50, 54, 58–9
printing, 13–14, 44, 50–4, 68–70
publishing, history of, 4, 6, 13, 17, 25, 38–40, 52–3, 63, 88n18. *See also* archives, publishers'
Purdy, Richard L., 24

Rabinowitz, Peter J., 77

race. *See* identity
Radway, Janice, 19
Raven, James, 13, 26, 33, 55, 57, 62, 66
reading, history of, 4, 6, 13–17, 21–3, 41–5, 55, 63, 67–9, 77
reading groups, 19
reception theory, 17, 19, 20, 75, 82n10
religion, history of, 24, 50, 65
Rose, Jonathan, 18, 85n30
Rubin, Joan Shelley, 87n26

St Clair, William, 22
science, history of, 13, 29, 41–5, 51–2, 65–6, 76
Secord, James, 13, 25, 41–5, 67, 71, 81n19
Sedo, DeNel R. *See* Fuller, Danielle, and DeNel R. Sedo
semasiographic. *See* sign systems
SHARP (Society for the History of Authorship, Reading and Publishing), 79n1
Sharpe, Kevin, 67–8, 75, 92n25
Shillingsburg, P.L., 21
sign systems, 57, 61
single book, history of a, 17, 24–5
sociology of texts. *See* bibliography
Steinberg, S.H., 88n17
Stiles, Lane. *See* Moylan, Michele, and Lane Stiles
Stoddard, Roger E., 20

Suleiman, Susan K., and Inge Crossman, 82n11
Sutherland, John, 8

Tanselle, G. Thomas, 32, 34, 84n30
teaching, 76–7
technological determinism, 48, 53–4, 56
television. *See* broadcast media
terminology, 5–6, 28, 34
text, 4, 11, 13, 15, 33–4, 38–40, 44–5, 51, 69. *See also* electronic texts; textual editing
textual editing, 11, 13, 20–1, 70–1
theory, 37–40; literary, 6, 27; of book culture, 4–5. *See also* new historicism
Thompson, E.P., 5
Topham, Jonathan, 51–2
transaction, book as a, 4, 33
Treadwell, Michael, 84n29

Vincent, David, 55

Walkowitz, Judith, 12, 47
Warkentin, Germaine, 61, 92n16
Webb, R.K., 82n7
Weedon, Alexis, 84n25
Winship, Michael, 25
women's history, 32, 46, 56–7
women's studies, 17, 19, 76

STUDIES IN BOOK AND PRINT CULTURE

General editor: Leslie Howsam

Hazel Bell, *Indexes and Indexing in Fact and Fiction*

Heather Murray, *Come, bright Improvement! The Literary Societies of Nineteenth-Century Ontario*

Joseph A. Dane, *The Myth of Print Culture: Essays on Evidence, Textuality, and Bibliographical Method*

Christopher J. Knight, *Uncommon Readers: Denis Donoghue, Frank Kermode, George Steiner, and the Tradition of the Common Reader*

Eva Hemmungs Wirtén, *No Trespassing: Authorship, Intellectual Property Rights, and the Boundaries of Globalization*

William A. Johnson, *Bookrolls and Scribes in Oxyrhynchus*

Siân Echard and Stephen Partridge, eds, *The Book Unbound: Editing and Reading Medieval Manuscripts and Texts*

Bronwen Wilson, *The World in Venice: Print, the City, and Early Modern Identity*

Peter Stoicheff and Andrew Taylor, eds, *The Future of the Page*

Jennifer Phegley and Janet Badia, eds, *Reading Women: Literary Figures and Cultural Icons from the Victorian Age to the Present*

Elizabeth Sauer, *'Paper-Contestations' and Textual Communities in England, 1640–1675*

Jonathan Carlyon, *Andrés González de Barcia and the Creation of the Colonial Spanish American Library*

Deborah McGrady, *Controlling Readers: Guillaume de Machaut and His Late Medieval Audience*

Bart Beaty, *Unpopular Culture: Transforming the European Comic Book in the 1990s*

Benjamin C. Withers, *The Illustrated Old English Hexateuch, Cotton Claudius B. iv: The Frontier of Seeing and Reading in Anglo-Saxon England*

Leslie Howsam, *Old Books and New Histories: An Orientation to Studies in Book and Print Culture*